GREAT SPORTING

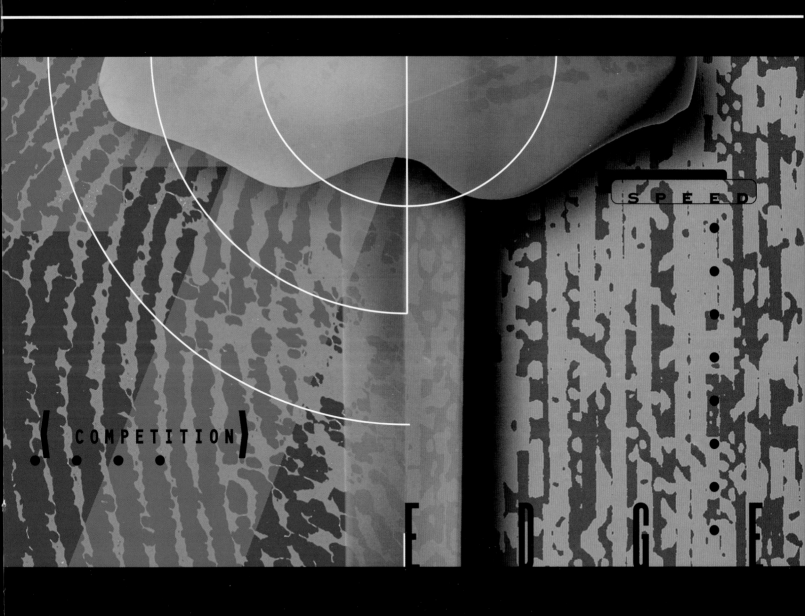

(COMPETITION)

SPEED

EDGE

GRAPHICS

First published in the United States of America by:
Rockport Publishers, Inc.
146 Granite Street
Rockport, Massachusetts 01966-1299
Telephone: (508) 546-9590
Fax: (508) 546-7141

Distributed to the book trade
and art trade in the U.S. by:
North Light, an imprint of
F & W Publications
1507 Dana Avenue
Cincinnati, Ohio 45207
Telephone: (513) 531-2222

Other Distribution by:
Rockport Publishers, Inc.
Rockport, Massachusetts 01966

ISBN 1-56496-179-6

10 9 8 7 6 5 4 3 2 1

Book Designer: H.A. Lind
Cover Designers: Jack Anderson, David Bates
Cover Photography: Tom Collicott

Printed in Singapore

GREAT SPORTING

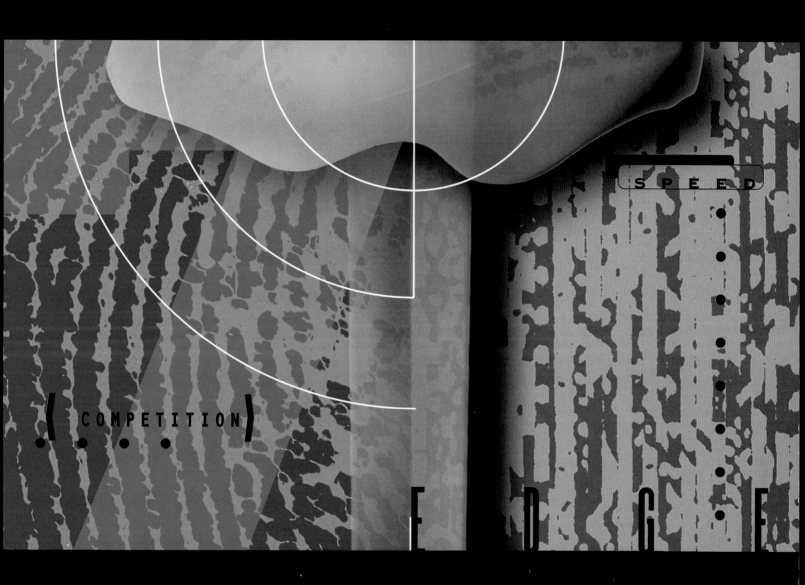

(COMPETITION)

SPEED

EDGE

GRAPHICS

ROCKPORT
PUBLISHERS

ROCKPORT PUBLISHERS
ROCKPORT, MASSACHUSETTS

TABLE OF CONTENTS

THE KEY TO
SPORTS GRAPHICS

BY JACK ANDERSON, PRINCIPAL
HORNALL ANDERSON DESIGN WORKS

**"Years ago, it was groovy.
Yesterday, extreme.
Today, it's fresh."**

The vocabulary adjusts for the moment. It changes to retain momentum and intrigue.

So it is with sports graphics the most ephemeral category in the world of graphic design. Unlike a corporate identity program that is created to have timeless appeal, sports graphics are seasonal. Temporary. They are created specifically for a brief existence. The designers involved are frequently deemed "on the cutting edge."

But what makes for successful sports graphics? How do you help manufacturers boost product sales? How do you know if the look you develop for the season will be a hit?

Like all areas of graphic design, there is a science behind the art. Specific criteria are discussed and established before design begins. Research into the sport and into the industry and its trends is crucial. After more than a decade of working with the marketing teams of top sports products manufacturers, our firm has developed several criteria that we automatically address during the design development process:

CREATE GRAPHICS THAT WORK IN TWO VERY DIFFERENT ENVIRONMENTS.
Sports graphics create the most marketing impact when developed to work in two very different environments. The selling environment offers an opportunity to distinguish the product from competing products and immediately affect the consumer's buying decision. The "use" environment plays an important marketing role by providing the chance to establish and to maintain the brand/product image. Reviewing the graphics' effectiveness in both environments is key to producing the hardest working and most successful images.

DEVELOP GRAPHICS TO ATTRACT TIGHTLY DEFINED TARGET MARKETS.
Every good designer knows that winning graphics are created to attract a certain audience. In sports graphics, this consideration must go one step further. Each product within a line must target a very specific consumer group. It isn't enough, anymore, to create a graphics program aimed at the generic bike rider. Today, products must be focused for the highly proficient mountain biker, or the weekend racing warrior, or the recreational street cyclist. The consumer's age, culture, and disposable income are all important considerations in the development of sports graphics.

TIE THE GRAPHICS IN WITH OTHER PRODUCTS IN THE SAME INDUSTRY.
Although the graphics must be unique, it is critical that the overall image and color palette correspond with other hard and soft goods products for the sport. Fashion-conscious consumers lead the pack in sales and demand that all components of their gear complement each other.

RESPECT THE INDUSTRIAL DESIGN FORM.
The graphics must enhance the technical benefits of the product structure. Technological features should be made readily apparent with graphic treatments. This makes the salesperson's challenge of highlighting the product's features much easier to meet.

BE A SPORTS ENTHUSIAST.
The more you understand about the art in each sport and its challenges, the more able you will be to create effective graphics. This understanding will help you reflect the action and intensity of the sport. Firsthand experience with the sport is definitely helpful. When possible, this experience will increase your understanding of the consumer's purchasing criteria.

CREATE AND MAINTAIN MARKET EQUITY.
As with all merchandising graphics, you must also create definite brand and product line awareness and leverage any existing market equity.

As an avid sports enthusiast, this is a category of graphic design that I find particularly appealing. The changing nature of the trends, the audiences, and their needs keeps our design team fresh and continues to push our skills and creativity to the next level. This stimulating process not only benefits our sports clients, it also keeps us growing and looking at all projects with a new perspective. The challenges of creating dynamic and successful sports graphics are great, and, with intense research, exploration, and creativity, the rewards are many.

5

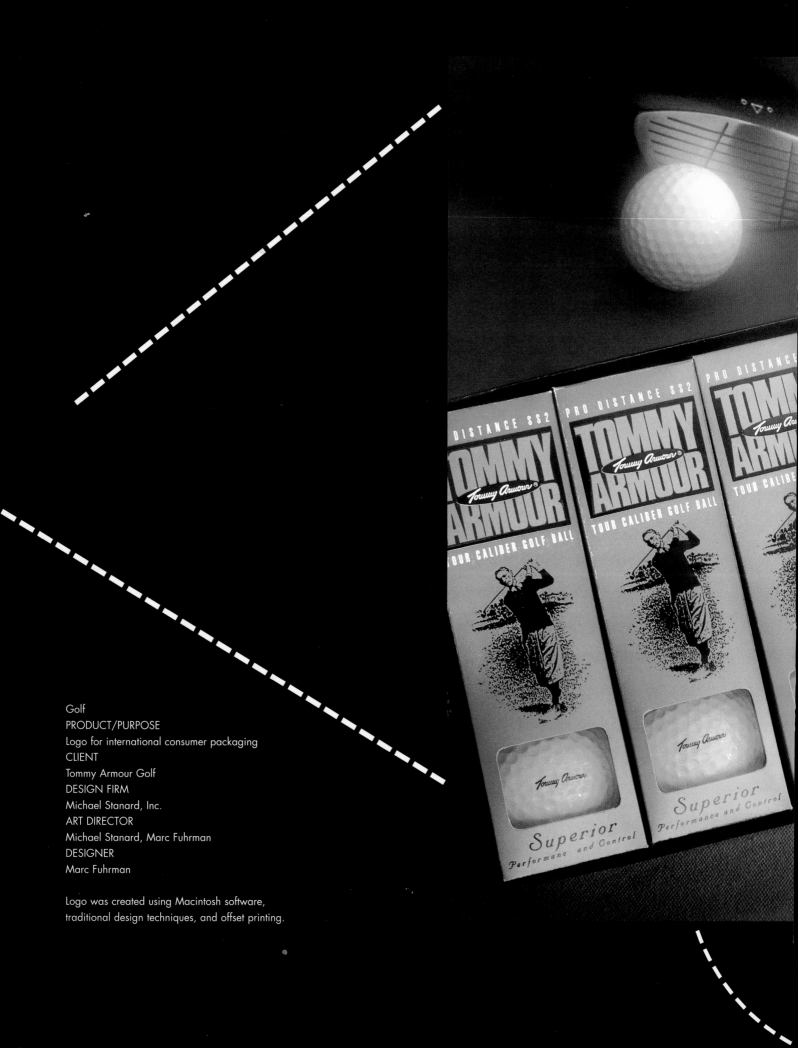

Golf
PRODUCT/PURPOSE
Logo for international consumer packaging
CLIENT
Tommy Armour Golf
DESIGN FIRM
Michael Stanard, Inc.
ART DIRECTOR
Michael Stanard, Marc Fuhrman
DESIGNER
Marc Fuhrman

Logo was created using Macintosh software,
traditional design techniques, and offset printing.

SWING IT

PRO DISTANCE SS2

TOMMY ARMOUR

TOUR CALIBER GOLF BALL

Pro Performance • 2-Piece Soft Surlyn® • Pro Sensitive Feel • Increased Spin and Control

Superior
Performance and Control

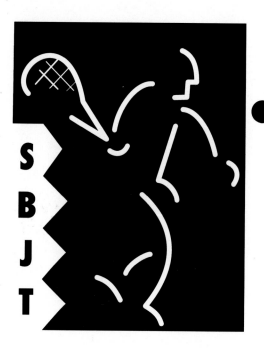

Tennis
PRODUCT/PURPOSE
Tennis group logo
CLIENT
South Bay Junior Tennis
DESIGN FIRM
Julia Tam Design
ALL DESIGN
Julia Chong Tam

Image was drawn by hand
and developed in Adobe Illustrator.

Tennis
PRODUCT/PURPOSE
Tennis racquet
CLIENT
Wilson Sporting Goods Company
DESIGN FIRM
Hornall Anderson Design Works
ART DIRECTOR
Jack Anderson
DESIGNER
Jack Anderson, Julie Lock

Design was created using
conventional methods.

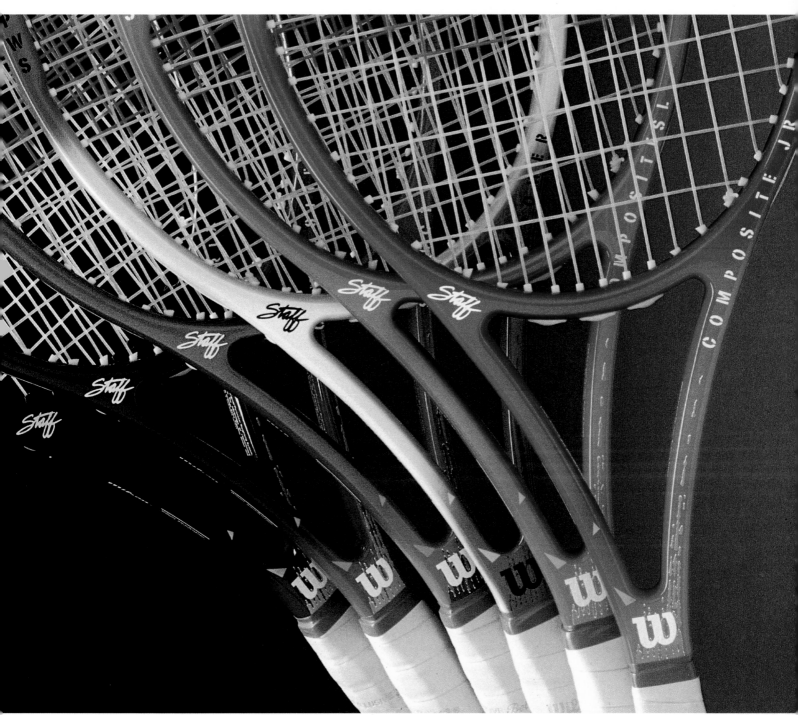

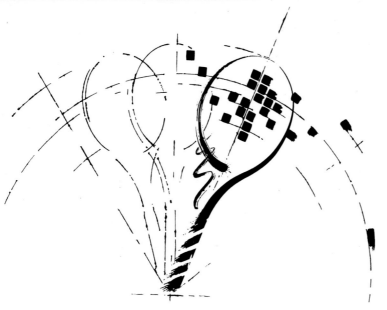

Tennis
PRODUCT/PURPOSE
United States Tennis Association logo
CLIENT
Cellular One
DESIGN FIRM
Hornall Anderson Design Works
ART DIRECTOR
Jack Anderson
DESIGNER
Jack Anderson, David Bates

Design created with a hand-drawn illustration
and a calligraphic brushstroke.

SWING IT

9

Baseball (Little League)
PRODUCT/PURPOSE
Baseball hats and other items
CLIENT
Little League Association
DESIGN FIRM
Anspach Grossman Portugal Inc.
ART DIRECTOR
Ken Love
DESIGNER
Amber Schowalter

Design created in Adobe Illustrator
and applied on various products.

Softball
PRODUCT/PURPOSE
Logo for uniforms
CLIENT
Hustlers Softball Team
DESIGN FIRM
Alfred Design
ALL DESIGN
John Alfred

Logo was created in Adobe Illustrator and was 2-color silk-screened on a softball jersey.

Baseball
PRODUCT/PURPOSE
Uniform logo
CLIENT
Tri-Star Pictures film *The Natural*
DESIGN FIRM
Mike Salisbury Communications Inc.
ART DIRECTOR
Mike Salisbury
DESIGNER
Dwight Smith
ILLUSTRATOR
Brian Sisson

Logo was applied to jackets, hats, and uniforms with embroidery.

Golf
PRODUCT/PURPOSE
Corporate identity
CLIENT
Golf Resort International
DESIGN FIRM
Cato Design Inc
DESIGNER
Andrew Stumpfel

Logo was created using Adobe
Illustrator. Offset printing was
used for the 2-color letterhead,
with the golf ball symbol white
foil-stamped.

Golf/Country Club Sports
PRODUCT/PURPOSE
Logo
CLIENT
DFS Group
DESIGN FIRM
Sackett Design Associates
DESIGNER
Mark Sackett, Wayne Sakamoto
ILLUSTRATOR
Mark Sackett, Wayne Sakamoto

A freehand drawing was scanned
into Adobe Photoshop and
combined with typography
using Adobe Illustrator
and QuarkXPress.

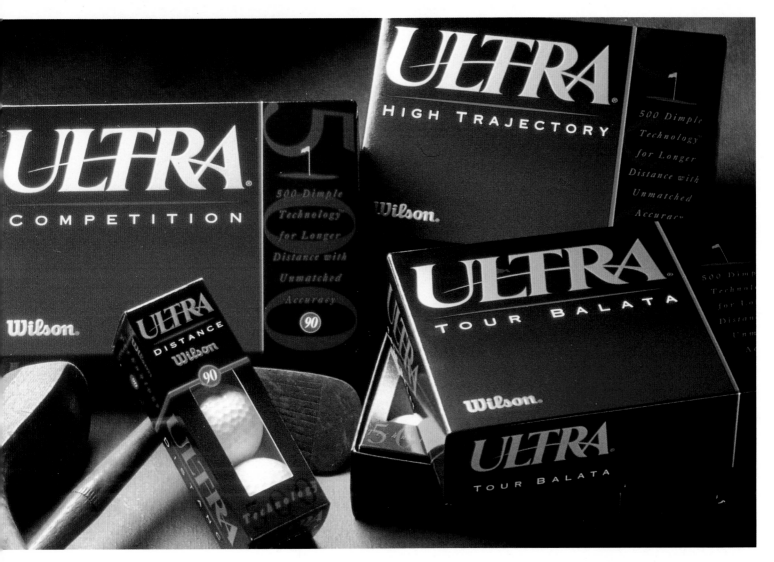

Golf
PRODUCT/PURPOSE
Golf ball packaging
CLIENT
Wilson Sporting Goods Company
DESIGN FIRM
Lipson-Alport-Glass & Associates
ART DIRECTOR
Sam J. Ciulla, Tracy Bacilek
DESIGNER
Andy Keene

This design system was created using Adobe Illustrator. The package structure was printed using offset lithography printing.

Golf
PRODUCT/PURPOSE
Logo for golf-influenced clothing store
CLIENT
Eaglemoor
DESIGN FIRM
Hornall Anderson Design Works

ART DIRECTOR
Jack Anderson
DESIGNER
Jack Anderson, Mary Hermes, David Bates
ILLUSTRATOR
Nancy Gellos

Logo was created traditionally.

Tennis
PRODUCT/PURPOSE
Tennis tournament promotional T-shirt
CLIENT
Clairol
DESIGN FIRM
Mike Quon Design Office
ART DIRECTOR
Mike Quon, Scott Fishoff
ALL DESIGN
Mike Quon

Illustration done by hand, scanned
into the computer, and colored in
Adobe Illustrator 5.5. Design was
printed on products with a
silk-screen process.

acquetball
RODUCT/PURPOSE
Gear bag and racquet
CLIENT
ktelon
ESIGN FIRM
Hires Design, Inc.
LL DESIGN
se Serrano

ut-amberlith art was scanned
nto the computer, re-drawn in
dobe Streamline 3.0, and
laced, along with the type,
nto Adobe Illustrator 3.2
or final output.

THE PLACE FOR HITTING IS AT HOME PLATE.

Baseball
PRODUCT/PURPOSE
Promotional Texas Rangers logo
CLIENT
Mental Health Association of Greate
Dallas
DESIGN FIRM
SullivanPerkins
ALL DESIGN
Art Garcia
PHOTOGRAPHY
Texas Ranger Archives

Street Hockey
PRODUCT/PURPOSE
Street Savage sportswear
CLIENT
Street Savage Sportswear
DESIGN FIRM
Swieter Design
ART DIRECTOR
John Swieter
DESIGNER
John Swieter, Mark Ford

Street hockey equipment logo
designed in Adobe Illustrator.

Softball
PRODUCT/PURPOSE
Wilson Fire Ball softball brochure
CLIENT
Wilson Sporting Goods
DESIGN FIRM
Qually + Co. Inc.
ALL DESIGN
Robert Qually
PHOTOGRAPHER
Peter Elliot

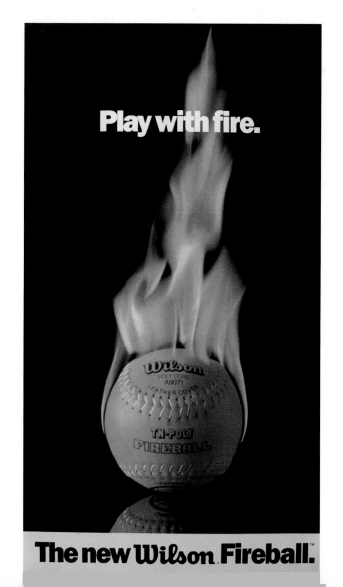

Play with fire.

The new Wilson Fireball.™

Golf
PRODUCT/PURPOSE
Retail products packaging
CLIENT
Korex Corporation
DESIGN FIRM
Michael Stanard, Inc.
ART DIRECTOR
Michael Stanard
DESIGNER
Marc Fuhrman

Created using Macintosh software,
traditional design techniques, and
offset and lithographic printing.

RUBBER
RUSH

KOREX
A DIAMOND IN THE ROUGH™
SPIKE WRENCH
DELUXE STEEL WITH PLASTIC HANDLE

KSW 5

KPS 30

Durable plastic counter
with key chain. Has
counter for strokes and
seperate counter for putts.

KOREX
A DIAMOND IN THE ROUGH™
PRO COUNT
WITH DURABLE KEY CHAIN

STROKES
73
COUNTER
92
PUTTS

E
ENCH

SPIKES

KUB 2

TY BRUSH
TO REPAIR GREENS

TIGHTENS ALL STAN

COUNTS UP TO 99 STROKES

KOREX
A DIAMOND IN THE

BALL
MARKERS

GOLF C

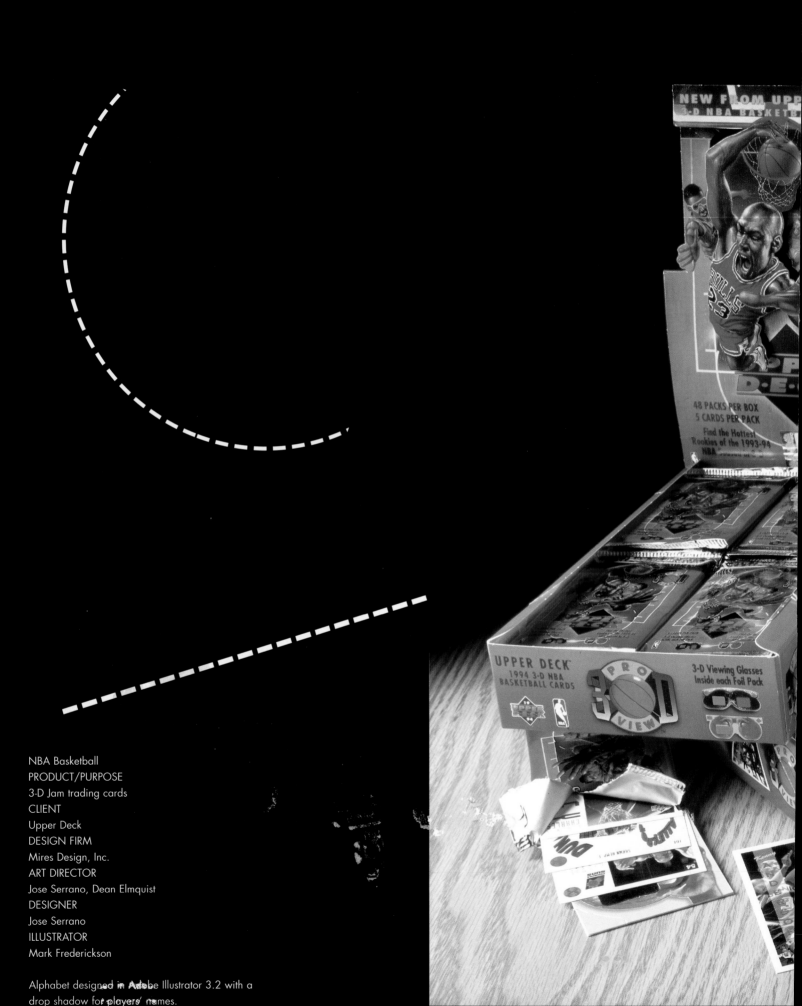

NBA Basketball
PRODUCT/PURPOSE
3-D Jam trading cards
CLIENT
Upper Deck
DESIGN FIRM
Mires Design, Inc.
ART DIRECTOR
Jose Serrano, Dean Elmquist
DESIGNER
Jose Serrano
ILLUSTRATOR
Mark Frederickson

Alphabet designed in Adobe Illustrator 3.2 with a
drop shadow for players' names.

PASS IT

Basketball
PRODUCT/PURPOSE
World Championship of Basketball in
Toronto logo
CLIENT
Toronto Professional Basketball
Organizing Committee
DESIGN FIRM
NBA Properties, Inc./Creative Services
ART DIRECTOR
Tom O'Grady
DESIGNER
Tom O'Grady
ILLUSTRATOR
William Reiser

Design created in Adobe Illustrator and
applied to merchandise in the form of
an embroidered patch.

Basketball
PRODUCT/PURPOSE
Sacramento Kings identity program
CLIENT
Sacramento Kings Professional Basketball Team
DESIGN FIRM
NBA Properties, Inc./Creative Services
ART DIRECTOR
Tom O'Grady
DESIGNER
Tom O'Grady
ILLUSTRATOR
Lux & Associates

This design was created in Adobe Illustrator. It was applied to the uniform with tackle twill lettering and embroidered patches.

Basketball
PRODUCT/PURPOSE
Phoenix Suns identity program
CLIENT
Phoenix Suns Professional Basketball Team
DESIGN FIRM
NBA Properties, Inc./Creative Services
ART DIRECTOR
Tom O'Grady
DESIGNER
Tom O'Grady
ILLUSTRATOR
Lux & Associates

This design was created in Adobe Illustrator
and applied to the uniforms with sublima-
tions, embroidery, and tackle twill lettering.

Basketball, Jamball
PRODUCT/PURPOSE
Basketball shoes, shoe box
CLIENT
FILA Footwear USA, Inc.
DESIGN FIRM
Kornick Lindsay
ART DIRECTOR
Sandy Krasovec

The character developed for the shoe was
drawn freehand, and the image was then
scanned into the computer and redrawn in
Adobe Illustrator. The logotype was screen-
printed on the boxes.

Basketball
PRODUCT/PURPOSE
Genuine leather logo
CLIENT
Tradeglobe Sports, Inc.
DESIGN FIRM
Swieter Design
ART DIRECTOR
John Swieter
DESIGNER
John Swieter, Kevin Flatt

Global identity created in Adobe Illustrator.

Basketball
PRODUCT/PURPOSE
Indoor/outdoor basketball packaging
CLIENT
Tradeglobe Sports, Inc.
DESIGN FIRM
Swieter Design
ART DIRECTOR
John Swieter
DESIGNER
John Swieter, Paul Munsterman

Design created in Abobe Illustrator.

Basketball
PRODUCT/PURPOSE
Genuine leather basketball packaging
CLIENT
Tradeglobe Sports, Inc.
DESIGN FIRM
Swieter Design
ART DIRECTOR
John Swieter
DESIGNER
John Swieter, Kevin Flatt

Product icon was created with Abobe Illustrator and features a global rendition of traditional basketball seams.

sketball
ODUCT/PURPOSE
curity Panel balls, packaging
IENT
adeglobe Sports, Inc.
SIGN FIRM
vieter Design
T DIRECTOR
hn Swieter
SIGNER
hn Swieter, Paul Munsterman

age created in Adobe Illustrator.

Basketball
PRODUCT/PURPOSE
All Converse basketball packaging
CLIENT
Tradeglobe Sports, Inc.
DESIGN FIRM
Swieter Design
ART DIRECTOR
John Swieter
DESIGNER
John Swieter, Paul Munsterman

The asphalt-like textures, street basketball
imagery, and product icons of this packaging were created in Adobe Illustrator.

asketball
RODUCT/PURPOSE
ecurity Panel logo
LIENT
adeglobe Sports, Inc.
ESIGN FIRM
wieter Design
T DIRECTOR
hn Swieter
ESIGNER
hn Swieter, Paul Munsterman
LUSTRATOR
evin Flatt

lobal identity created in Adobe Illustrator.

Football
PRODUCT/PURPOSE
FIFA Fair Play trophy, logo
CLIENT
ISL Marketing, FIFA
DESIGN FIRM
Pentagram Design
ALL DESIGN
Michael Gericke

The design was initially created
in three-dimensional clay models;
fabrication drawing was then
done on a Macintosh computer.

Football
PRODUCT/PURPOSE
Tournament Poster
CLIENT
Camara Municipal Do Porto
DESIGN FIRM
Mário Aurélio & Associados

ART DIRECTOR
Mário Aurélio
DESIGNER
Mário Aurélio, Rosa Maia

Design was created using a combination of Aldus FreeHand, Apple Print, and screen-printing programs.

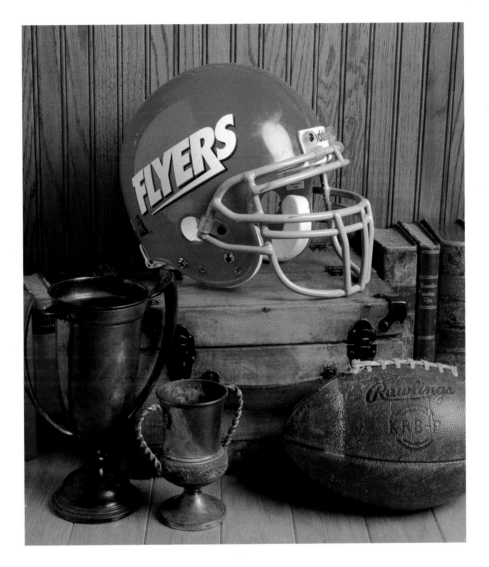

American Football
PRODUCT/PURPOSE
University of Dayton football helmet
CLIENT
University of Dayton
DESIGN FIRM
Rickabaugh Graphics
ALL DESIGN
Eric Rickabaugh

The Dayton Flyers logo was created in Aldus
FreeHand.

Basketball
PRODUCT/PURPOSE
Shoe store promotional T-shirt
CLIENT
Kinney Corporation
DESIGN FIRM
Mike Quon Design Office
ALL DESIGN
Mike Quon

Illustration done by hand, scanned into
the computer, and colored in Adobe
Illustrator 5.5. Design was printed on
products with a silk-screen process.

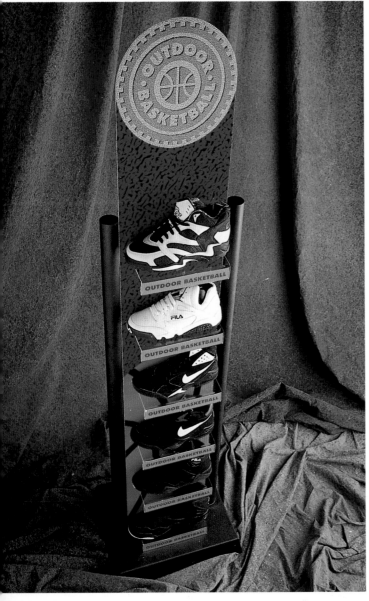

Basketball
PRODUCT/PURPOSE
Basketball shoe tower
CLIENT
FootAction USA
DESIGN FIRM
Swieter Design
ART DIRECTOR
John Swieter
DESIGNER
John Swieter, Jenice Heo

Image created in Adobe Photoshop and
imported into Adobe Illustrator.

Basketball
PRODUCT/PURPOSE
Toronto Raptors identity program
CLIENT
Toronto Raptors Professional Basketball Organization
DESIGN FIRM
NBA Properties, Inc./Creative Services
ART DIRECTOR
Tom O'Grady
DESIGNER
Ed O'Hara, Andrew Blanco

Design created using Adobe Illustrator. Sublimation, embroidery, and tackle twill lettering were used to apply the design to items.

© 1994 NBAP

PASS IT

33

Football
PRODUCT/PURPOSE
Identity for Champions League
CLIENT
UEFA
DESIGN FIRM
Design Bridge Limited
ART DIRECTOR
Rob Petrie
DESIGNER
Phil Clements, Marion Dalley, Mike Harris

Desktop software for Apple Macintosh was used in
the design process.

American Football
PRODUCT/PURPOSE
Double Trouble poster
CLIENT
Dallas Cowboys Football
Organization
DESIGN FIRM
Swieter Design
ART DIRECTOR
John Swieter
DESIGNER
John Swieter, Paul Munsterman,
Kevin Flatt

Design created with Abode
Illustrator.

American Football
PRODUCT/PURPOSE
Mascot logo
CLIENT
University of Indianapolis Athletic
Department (Greyhounds)
DESIGN FIRM
Dean Johnson Design
ALL DESIGN
Mike Schwab

Market drawings were scanned into
a Macintosh computer and refined in
Aldus FreeHand for linotronic output,
which was then produced into decals
for helmets.

American Football
PRODUCT/PURPOSE
Dallas Cowboys leather portfolio
CLIENT
Dallas Cowboys Football Organization
DESIGN FIRM
Swieter Design
ALL DESIGN
John Swieter

The logo for this portfolio was developed
in Adobe Illustrator.

Basketball
PRODUCT/PURPOSE
University of Dayton Flyers basketball court graphics
CLIENT
University of Dayton
DESIGN FIRM
Rickabaugh Graphics
ALL DESIGN
Eric Rickabaugh

The floor graphics were created in Aldus FreeHand and then projected up and transferred by hand onto a carbon-backed paper. The paper was transferred to the floor, masked with tape, and painted by hand.

Rugby
PRODUCT/PURPOSE
Identity for sponsorship of season by ITV/Scottish Provident
CLIENT
ITV Sport
DESIGN FIRM
Design Bridge Limited
ART DIRECTOR
Rod Petrie
DESIGNER
Mike Harris

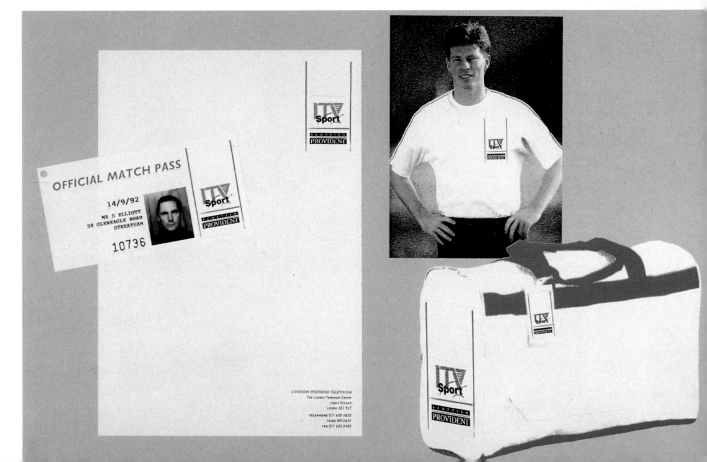

Mountain Biking
PRODUCT/PURPOSE
Merchandising items for bike fair
CLIENT
Brasbike Comércio De Imp. e Exp. Ltda.
DESIGN FIRM
Animus Comunicação
ART DIRECTOR
Rique Nitzsche
DESIGNER
Felício Torres

The logo was drawn using the
CorelDraw 4.0 software and silk-
screened on T-shirts. The folder was offset printed. The material, including the
brand of the company, was used at a
U.S. bike fair and had to be produced,
from the layout to finished material, in
three days.

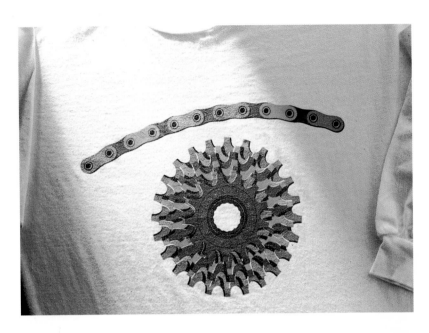

Cycling
PRODUCT/PURPOSE
T-Shirt
DESIGN FIRM
Hornall Anderson Design Works
ART DIRECTOR
Jack Anderson
DESIGNER
Julie Keenan
ILLUSTRATOR
Julie Keenan, John Anicker

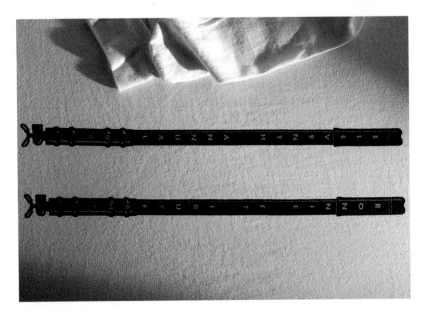

Skateboarding
PRODUCT/PURPOSE
Point of purchase poster
CLIENT
Vans Shoes, Inc.
DESIGN FIRM
dGWB Advertising
ART DIRECTOR
Wade Koniakowsky
DESIGNER
Jeff Labbé
ILLUSTRATOR
Janice Lowry

Design created with Adobe Photoshop 3.0.

Root River Trail

Cycling
PRODUCT/PURPOSE
Promotion of bike trail
CLIENT
Root River Trail Association
DESIGN FIRM
Design Center
ART DIRECTOR
John Reger
DESIGNER
Sherwin Swartzrock

The design was rendered in Aldus FreeHand, and type was set using a Macintosh computer. The symbol has been well received and will eventually be used on stationery, trail signs, and vehicles.

Cycling
PRODUCT/PURPOSE
Bicycle helmets, accessories, packaging
CLIENT
Giro Sport Design, Inc.
DESIGN FIRM
Hornall Anderson Design Works
ART DIRECTOR
Jack Anderson
DESIGNER
Jack Anderson, David Bates, Lian Ng

Design created in Aldus FreeHand and Adobe Photoshop.
Helmets were silk-screened with three to eight passes on the
backside of plastic sheeting. The sheeting was vacuformed
to the helmet shape, trimmed out, and attached to helmets.

Cycling
PRODUCT/PURPOSE
Race team logo
CLIENT
Gang of Seven
DESIGN FIRM
Hornall Anderson Design Works
ART DIRECTOR
Jack Anderson
DESIGNER
Jack Anderson, Brian O'Neill

Logo was created in Aldus FreeHand and
silk-screened onto pre-made jerseys.

Cycling
PRODUCT/PURPOSE
Bicycles
CLIENT
Davidson Cycles
DESIGN FIRM
Hornall Anderson Design Works
ART DIRECTOR
Jack Anderson
DESIGNER
Jack Anderson, Mary Hermes,
Jani Drewfs
ILLUSTRATOR
David Bates, Scott McDougall

Design created conventionally.
Photographs shot with multiple
exposures, and airbrushing was
used for the zig-zag effects.

Cycling
PRODUCT/PURPOSE
Bicycle store logo
CLIENT
Los Gatos Cyclery
DESIGN FIRM
THARP DID IT
ART DIRECTOR
Rick Tharp
DESIGNER
Rick Tharp, Laurie Okamura

Cycling
PRODUCT/PURPOSE
T-shirt, poster
CLIENT
Core States
DESIGN FIRM
Hanson Associates, Inc.
ART DIRECTOR
Gil Hanson
DESIGNER
Tobin Beck

The design was formulated through
a combination of hand drawing
and manipulations in Adobe
Illustrator and Adobe Photoshop on
a Macintosh computer.

Cycling
PRODUCT/PURPOSE
Bicycles, accessories
CLIENT
Raleigh Cycle Company of America
DESIGN FIRM
Hornall Anderson Design Works
ART DIRECTOR
Jack Anderson
DESIGNER
Jack Anderson, David Bates, John Anicker, Mary Chin Hutchinson, Julie Keenan

Design for this bicycle logo was created conventionally. The product catalog was designed in QuarkXPress and Adobe Photoshop.

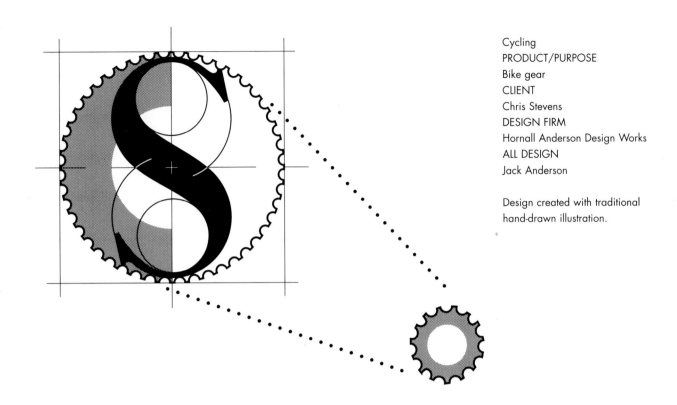

Cycling
PRODUCT/PURPOSE
Bike gear
CLIENT
Chris Stevens
DESIGN FIRM
Hornall Anderson Design Works
ALL DESIGN
Jack Anderson

Design created with traditional
hand-drawn illustration.

Cycling
PRODUCT/PURPOSE
Bicycle wheel graphics
CLIENT
Spinergy, Inc.
DESIGN FIRM
Clifford Selbert Design Collaborative
ART DIRECTOR
Robin Perkins
DESIGNER
Robin Perkins, Jeff Breidenbach

QuarkXPress and Aldus FreeHand
were used in the design process.

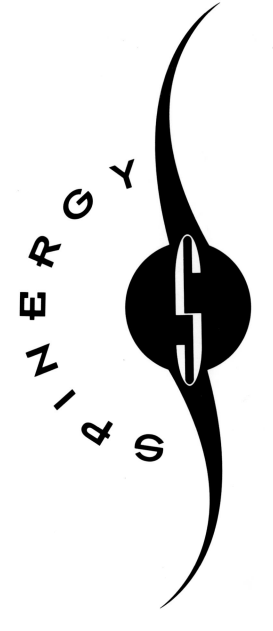

Cycling
PRODUCT/PURPOSE
Corporate identity
CLIENT
Spinergy, Inc.
DESIGN FIRM
Clifford Selbert Design Collaborative
ALL DESIGN
Robin Perkins

QuarkXPress and Aldus FreeHand were
used to create this corporate identity,
which is found on an array of Spinergy
products.

Car Racing
PRODUCT/PURPOSE
Race car logo
CLIENT
Texaco
DESIGN FIRM
Anspach Grossman Portugal Inc.
ART DIRECTOR
Ken Love
DESIGNER
Glenn Stockton

Created in Adobe Illustrator and applied
as a 3M decal to the car.

Car Racing
PRODUCT/PURPOSE
Uniform logo
CLIENT
Texaco
DESIGN FIRM
Anspach Grossman Portugal, Inc.
ART DIRECTOR
Ken Love
DESIGNER
Amber Schowalter

Created in Adobe Illustrator and applied
as decals and sewn to uniforms.

Cycling
PRODUCT/PURPOSE
Bicycle specialty store logo
CLIENT
Two Wheel Transit Authority
DESIGN FIRM
Byron Jacobs Design
ALL DESIGN
Byron Jacobs

This logo/corporate identity was created with free-hand drawing. The logo was applied by many methods, including offset printing, screen-printing, and decals.

ateboarding
ODUCT/PURPOSE
irts, skateboards
IENT
gDog
SIGN FIRM
ke Salisbury Communications Inc.
T DIRECTOR
ke Salisbury
SIGNER
ke Salisbury
USTRATOR
an Sisson

is design was computer embroi-
red on shirts, and silk-screened
skateboards.

BMX Biking
PRODUCT/PURPOSE
Pimentinha BMX identity T-shirt
CLIENT
A.C. Pimenta (Pimentinha)
DESIGN FIRM
Antero Ferreira Design
ART DIRECTOR
Antero Ferreira
DESIGNER
Joana Alves
ILLUSTRATOR
Eduardo Sotto Mayor

Design was created through traditional
drawing, as well as with Aldus
FreeHand 3.1.1 to introduce the colors.

Cycling
PRODUCT/PURPOSE
Bicycle equipment
CLIENT
Cascade Bicycle Club
DESIGN FIRM
Hornall Anderson Design Works
ART DIRECTOR
Jack Anderson
DESIGNER
Jack Anderson, Jani Drewfs, David Bates

Design created by hand with splatter-stripple artwork and intentional moire pattern.

MX Biking, Mountain Biking,
In-Line Skating
PRODUCT/PURPOSE
Apparel
CLIENT
Torque Center USA
DESIGN FIRM
Rocket Advertising Design
ALL DESIGN
Eric Timm

Cycling
PRODUCT/PURPOSE
Bicycle rack fairing
DESIGN FIRM
Thule

Logo was silk-screened onto a lexan shield.

rcling
ODUCT/PURPOSE
ir bicycle rack
SIGN FIRM
ule

Cycling
PRODUCT/PURPOSE
Brochure
CLIENT
Shimano Bicycles
DESIGN FIRM
dGWB Advertising
ART DIRECTOR
Joe Cladis, Wade Kiniakowsky
ILLUSTRATOR
Kevin Short, Johnny Bee

Design developed in QuarkXPress 3.3,
and Adobe Photoshop 2.5.

MCMXCIIII

$2.50 COMPLIMENTARY

california
active
THe GUIDe TO HeALTH, SPORTS & FITNeSS

it's getting
hotter and hotter

run for yourself

line up to
skate
line up to
skate

walking
tough

my own gym
how to camp with your car
bikes, bytes and boots

Cycling
PRODUCT/PURPOSE
Bicycles, accessories
CLIENT
Raleigh Cycle Company of America
DESIGN FIRM
Hornall Anderson Design Works
ART DIRECTOR
Jack Anderson
DESIGNER
Jack Anderson, David Bates, John
Anicker, Mary Chin Hutchinson,
Julie Keenan

Design for bicycle logo was created
conventionally.

In-Line Skating
PRODUCT/PURPOSE
Magazine cover design
CLIENT
Cal Active
DESIGN FIRM
Mike Salisbury Communications Inc.
ART DIRECTOR
Mike Salisbury
DESIGNER
Regina Grosveld
ILLUSTRATOR
Fosbrook Passo (photo)

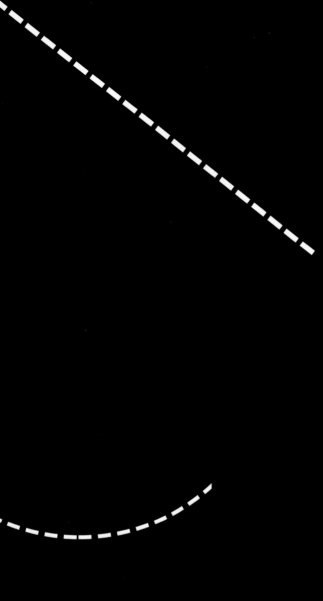

Windsurfing
PRODUCT/PURPOSE
Product development, corporate
identity
CLIENT
Tiga/Neil Pryde
DESIGN FIRM
PPA Design Limited
ALL DESIGN
Byron Jacobs

Desktop software used was Aldus
FreeHand and QuarkXPress. Offset
printing, screen-printing, decals, and
video were also used in the design
process.

MAKE A WA

Windsurfing
PRODUCT/PURPOSE
Product development, corporate identity
CLIENT
Tiga/Neil Pryde
DESIGN FIRM
PPA Design Limited
ALL DESIGN
Byron Jacobs

Aldus FreeHand and QuarkXPress were used in the
design process.

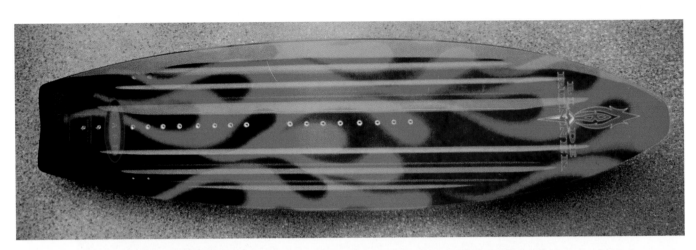

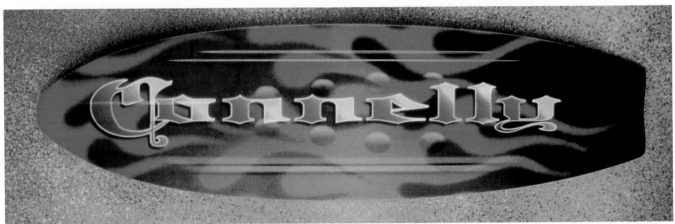

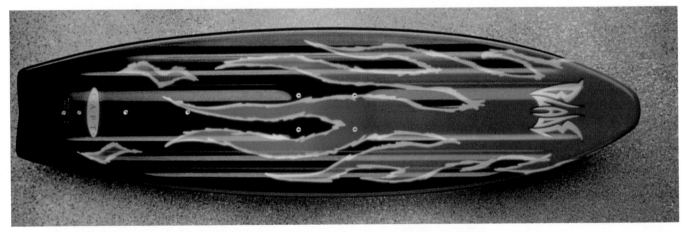

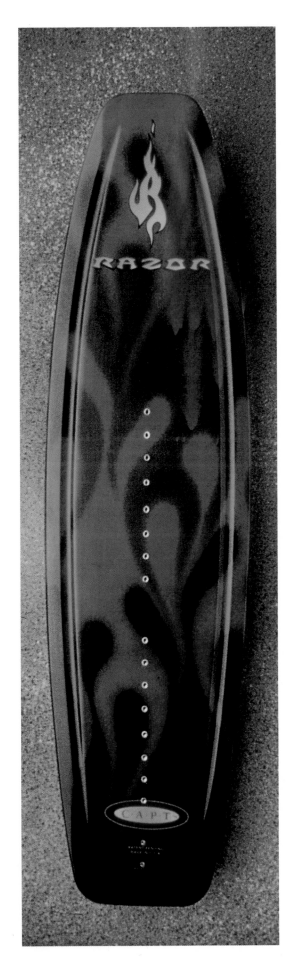

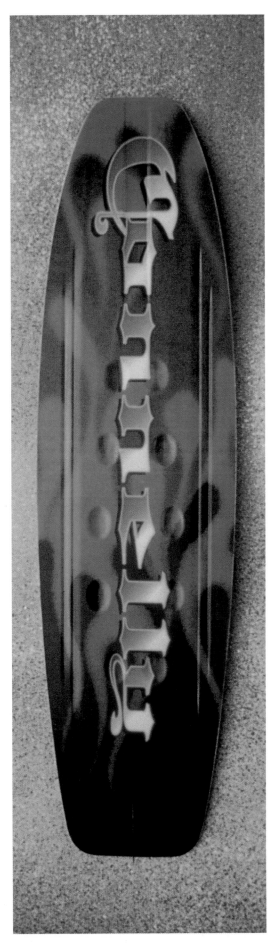

ake Boarding
ODUCT/PURPOSE
zor, Blade Runner, Blade boards
IENT
nnelly Water Skis
SIGN FIRM
th Floor
T DIRECTOR
c Ruffing
SIGNER
ve Parmley, Eric Ruffing
USTRATOR
ve Parmley, Eric Ruffing

age was created in Aldus
eeHand 4.0, brought into Adobe
otoshop 2.5, and treated in KPT
yce Texture Explorer. Design was
oduced by dye-sublimation and
raviolet lamination.

Surfing
PRODUCT/PURPOSE
Surf trunks
CLIENT
MCD
DESIGN FIRM
Mike Salisbury Communications Inc.
ALL DESIGN
Mike Salisbury

This street-edge surf logo was handwoven
and embroidered.

Surfing
PRODUCT/PURPOSE
"Animal" wetsuit
CLIENT
O'Neill Wetsuits
DESIGN FIRM
13th Floor
ART DIRECTOR
Dave Parmley
DESIGNER
Dave Parmley, Eric Ruffing, Tim Ward

All these logos were comped by hand and
then scanned. Templates were cleaned
and readied in Aldus FreeHand 2.0. The
Jack O'Neill and OXS logos were output
to film and made into PVC patches that
were glued onto the suit. Since this suit
has 3-D stretch panels, graphics were
applied in a dimensional way. The other
logos were silk-screened with a propri-
etary ink that O'Neill developed.

Skiing
PRODUCT/PURPOSE
Skis, hangtags, accessories
CLIENT
K2 Corporation
DESIGN FIRM
Hornall Anderson Design Works
ART DIRECTOR
Jack Anderson
DESIGNER
Jack Anderson, Mary Hermes, John Anicker, Brian O'Neill, David Bates, Jani Drewfs, Denise Weir

Design created in Aldus FreeHand and Adobe Photoshop. Graphics and type were developed in a single program and were placed directly from Photoshop.

Skiing
PRODUCT/PURPOSE
Skis, accessories
CLIENT
K2 Corporation
DESIGN FIRM
Hornall Anderson Design Works
ART DIRECTOR
Jack Anderson
DESIGNER
Jack Anderson, Denise Weir, Julie
Lock, Jani Drewfs
ILLUSTRATOR
Denise Weir, Jani Drewfs

Design created and developed
in Aldus FreeHand and Adobe
Photoshop.

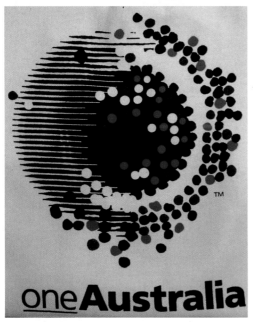

Sailing
PRODUCT/PURPOSE
One Australia America's Cup Challenge logo
CLIENT
One Australia
DESIGN FIRM
Cato Design Inc
ALL DESIGN
Ken Cato

Logo was computer-generated using Adobe Illustrator and applied to the hull of the boat by hand. Screen-printed promotional banners and garments were also part of this campaign. The One Australia symbol combines an image of strong technological resources with Australian cultural design elements.

Surfing
PRODUCT/PURPOSE
Surfboard
CLIENT
Croteau Surfboards
DESIGN FIRM
Russell Leong Design
ALL DESIGN
Russell Leong

The design was airbrushed directly
on the surfboard.

Surfing
PRODUCT/PURPOSE
Surfboard
CLIENT
Santa Cruz Surf Shop
DESIGN FIRM
Russell Leong Design
ART DIRECTOR
Russell Leong
DESIGNER
Russell Leong
ILLUSTRATOR
Emiko Oyama

The design was airbrushed directly on a
surfboard core foam.

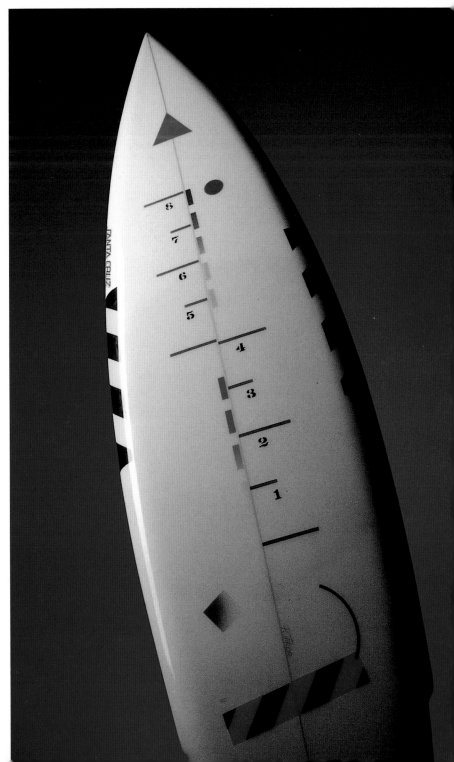

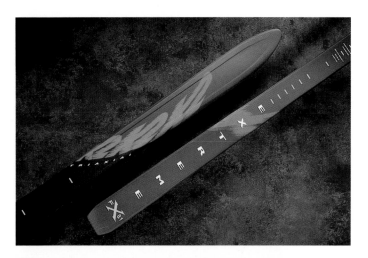

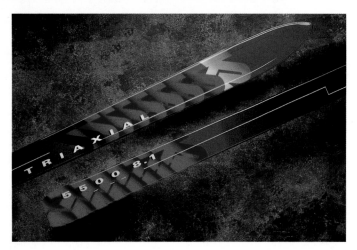

Skiing
PRODUCT/PURPOSE
Skis, hangtags, accessories
CLIENT
K2 Corporation
DESIGN FIRM
Hornall Anderson Design Works
ART DIRECTOR
Jack Anderson
DESIGNER
Jack Anderson, Mary Hermes, John Anicker, Brian
O'Neill, David Bates, Jani Drewfs, Denise Weir

Design created in Aldus FreeHand and Adobe Photoshop.

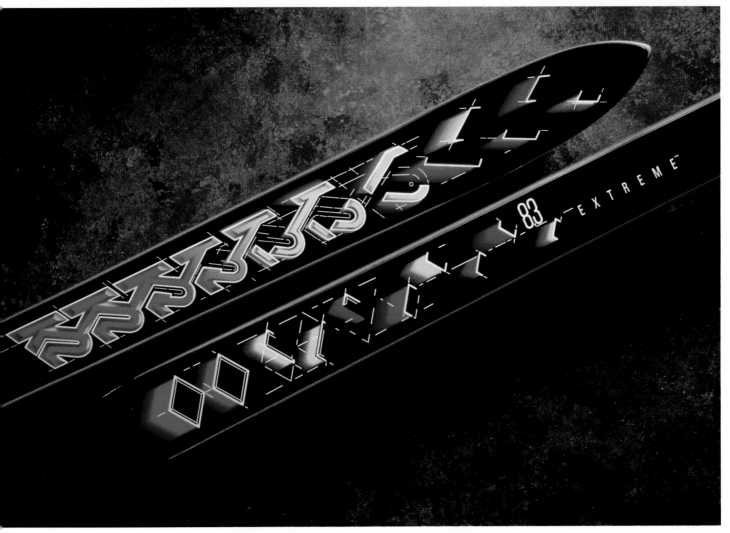

Windsurfing
PRODUCT/PURPOSE
Windsurfing product catalog
CLIENT
Tiga Windsurfing Boards and Sails
DESIGN FIRM
PPA Design Limited
ART DIRECTOR
Byron Jacobs
DESIGNER
Byron Jacobs, Tracy Hou

Developed with Aldus PageMaker, Aldus FreeHand, and offset printing, this image was designed to give the company a new identity.

Windsurfing
PRODUCT/PURPOSE
Windsurfing product catalog
CLIENT
Neil Pryde
DESIGN FIRM
PPA Design Limited
ART DIRECTOR
Byron Jacobs
DESIGNER
Byron Jacobs, Bernard Lau
ILLUSTRATOR
Bob Franklin

Images were developed with Aldus
PageMaker, Aldus FreeHand, and offset
printing. The catalog's theme is techno-
logically advanced equipment and
accessories. Sail designs are created
and refined with the help of a CAD-
CAM program.

Skiing
PRODUCT/PURPOSE
Skis, accessories
CLIENT
K2 Corporation
DESIGN FIRM
Hornall Anderson Design Works
ART DIRECTOR
Jack Anderson
DESIGNER
Jack Anderson, Denise Weir, Julie
Lock, Jani Drewfs
ILLUSTRATOR
Denise Weir, Jani Drewfs

Design created in Aldus FreeHand
and Adobe Photoshop. Type and
graphics were developed in a single
program and files were placed from
Photoshop.

Skiing
PRODUCT/PURPOSE
Skis, hangtags, accessories
CLIENT
K2 Corporation
DESIGN FIRM
Hornall Anderson Design
Works
ART DIRECTOR
Jack Anderson
DESIGNER
Jack Anderson, Mary Hermes,
John Anicker, Brian O'Neill,
David Bates, Jani Drewfs,
Denise Weir

Design created in Aldus
FreeHand and Adobe
Photoshop.

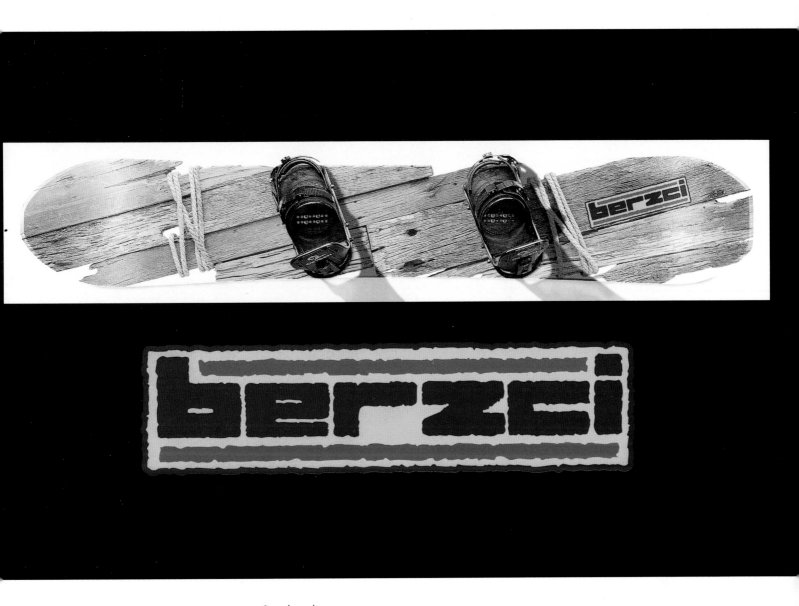

Snowboarding
PRODUCT/PURPOSE
Board logo
CLIENT
Elton Ward Design
DESIGN FIRM
Elton Ward Design
ART DIRECTOR
Steve Coleman
DESIGNER
Simon Macrae
PHOTOGRAPHER
Andrew Kay
ARTIST
Andrew Schipp

Flat timber was photographed as a texture base.
Bindings were shot separately and later added to
the ski. The ski image was entirely constructed in
Adobe Photoshop. Shadows were airbrushed, and
the background was airbrushed with added filters.

Surfing
PRODUCT/PURPOSE
Pimentinha Surfer T-shirt
CLIENT
A.C. Pimenta (Pimentinha)
DESIGN FIRM
Antero Ferreira Design
ART DIRECTOR
Antero Ferreira
DESIGNER
Joana Alves
ILLUSTRATOR
Eduardo Sotto Mayor

Design was created through
traditional drawing, as well as
with Aldus FreeHand 3.1.1 to
introduce the colors.

Swimming
PRODUCT/PURPOSE
Swim flotation packaging
CLIENT
Gopher Swim Wear
DESIGN FIRM
Elton Ward Design
ART DIRECTOR
Steve Coleman
DESIGNER
Chris De Lisen
PHOTOGRAPHER
Anthony Brown

Logo and packaging graphics
were hand-illustrated and
scanned as a template into
Adobe Illustrator where they were
built, colorized, and refined for
final separations.

Surfing
PRODUCT/PURPOSE
Surfboard Carrier
DESIGN FIRM
Thule

Surfing
PRODUCT/PURPOSE
Surfing label
CLIENT
Birdwell
DESIGN FIRM
Mike Salisbury Communications Inc.
ALL DESIGN
Mike Salisbury

This design was hand-drawn with a
speedball pen; the lettering was created
using handcut Rubylith.

Surfing
PRODUCT/PURPOSE
Clothing
CLIENT
Gotcha
DESIGN FIRM
Mike Salisbury
Communications Inc.
ALL DESIGN
Mike Salisbury

Snowboarding
PRODUCT/PURPOSE
Jacket
CLIENT
GOTCHA
DESIGN FIRM
Mike Salisbury
Communications Inc.
ALL DESIGN
Mike Salisbury

Silk-screen and embroidery were
used in this design creation.

Skiing/Multipurpose
PRODUCT/PURPOSE
Adventurer equipment carrier
CLIENT
Thule
DESIGN FIRM
Erin Edwards Advertising

Designed with desktop publishing software. This design is a die-cut decal applied to the box just before it is packed in the shipping carton.

Skiing
PRODUCT/PURPOSE
Skis
CLIENT
PRE Skis
DESIGN FIRM
Studio M D
ART DIRECTOR
Jesse Doquillo, Randy Lim,
Glenn Mitsui
DESIGNER
Jesse Doquillo, Randy Lim

Artwork created using Aldus FreeHand and Adobe Photoshop. Design was screen-printed on the back of special, transparent plastics.

Skiing
PRODUCT/PURPOSE
Gondola car
CLIENT
Killington, Ltd.
DESIGN FIRM
PandaMonium Designs
ART DIRECTOR
Raymond Yu
DESIGNER
Steven Lee, Raymond Yu
ILLUSTRATOR
Steven Lee, Raymond Yu,
Deena Prestegard

Surfing
PRODUCT/PURPOSE
Advertisement
CLIENT
Ocean Pacific
DESIGN FIRM
Mike Salisbury Communications Inc.
ART DIRECTOR
Mike Salisbury
DESIGNER
Mike Salisbury, Terry Lamb
ILLUSTRATOR
Terry Lamb

Surfing
PRODUCT/PURPOSE
Catalog
CLIENT
Gotcha
DESIGN FIRM
Mike Salisbury Communications Inc.
ART DIRECTOR
Mike Salisbury
DESIGNER
Mike Salisbury
ILLUSTRATOR
Terry Lamb, Pat Linse, Patrick O'Neil
Pam Hamilton, Mike Finn (photo),
Elizabeth Salisbury

Logo created by hand, without the u
of computers. The lettering and illust
tion were collaged on color laser
copies.

Skiing
PRODUCT/PURPOSE
Skis, hangtags, accessories
CLIENT
K2 Corporation
DESIGN FIRM
Hornall Anderson Design Works
ART DIRECTOR
Jack Anderson
DESIGNER
Jack Anderson, Mary Hermes, John
Anicker, Brian O'Neill, David Bates,
Jani Drewfs, Denise Weir

Design created in Aldus FreeHand
and Adobe Photoshop.

Snowboarding
PRODUCT/PURPOSE
Snowboard
CLIENT
Norteca Sports
DESIGN FIRM
Russell Leong Design
ALL DESIGN
Russell Leong

Image was created by conventional
drawing, Xerography, and screen-
printing.

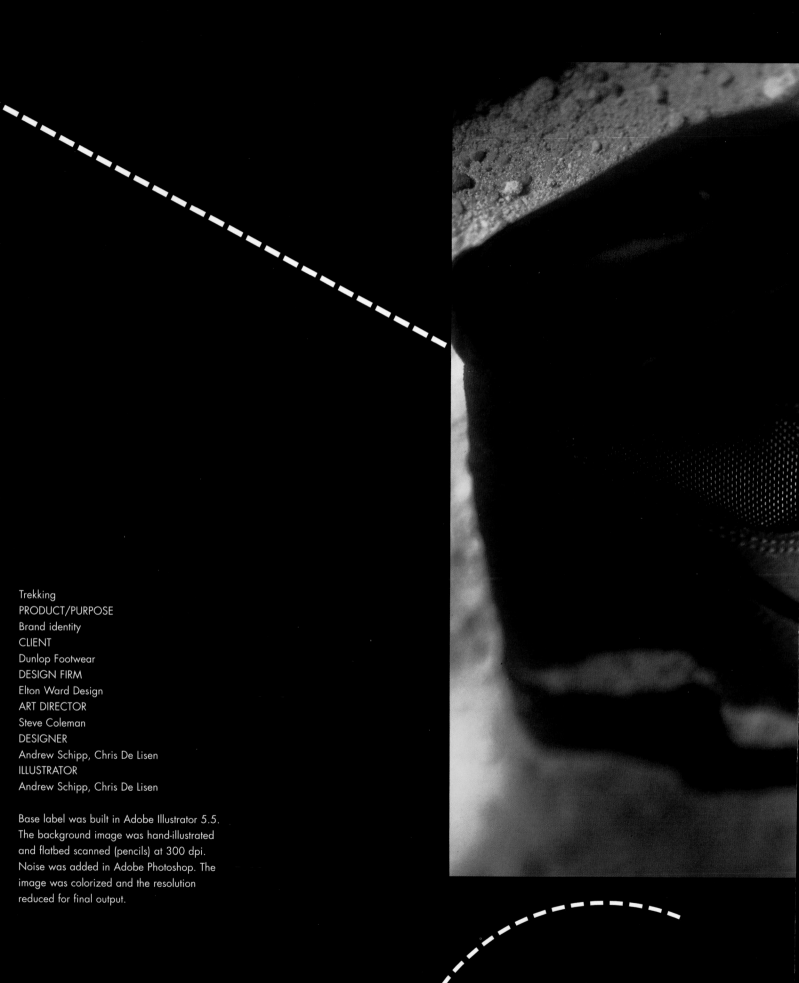

Trekking
PRODUCT/PURPOSE
Brand identity
CLIENT
Dunlop Footwear
DESIGN FIRM
Elton Ward Design
ART DIRECTOR
Steve Coleman
DESIGNER
Andrew Schipp, Chris De Lisen
ILLUSTRATOR
Andrew Schipp, Chris De Lisen

Base label was built in Adobe Illustrator 5.5.
The background image was hand-illustrated
and flatbed scanned (pencils) at 300 dpi.
Noise was added in Adobe Photoshop. The
image was colorized and the resolution
reduced for final output.

OUT OF BOUNDS

DUNLOP

TREKKING

BUILT FROM INDUSTRIAL
HERITAGE & SPORTING
TECHNOLOGY

Hiking
PRODUCT/PURPOSE
Hiking shoe tower
CLIENT
FootAction USA
DESIGN FIRM
Swieter Design
ART DIRECTOR
John Swieter
DESIGNER
Paul Munsterman
ILLUSTRATOR
Paul Munsterman

The chart, map, and compass imagery of this logo, created in Adobe Illustrator and Adobe Photoshop, emphasizes the challenges of exploring the Great Outdoors.

Running
PRODUCT/PURPOSE
ASICS shoe tower
CLIENT
FootAction USA
DESIGN FIRM
Swieter Design
ART DIRECTOR
John Swieter
DESIGNER
Jenice Heo
ILLUSTRATOR
Jenice Heo

Fishing
PRODUCT/PURPOSE
Fishing line packaging
CLIENT
Remington Arms Company, Inc.
DESIGN FIRM
Lipson-Alport-Glass & Associates
ART DIRECTOR
Sam J. Ciulla
DESIGNER
Lyle Zimmerman

Design created using Adobe Illustrator. The
package structure was printed using offset
lithography printing.

Kite Flying
PRODUCT/PURPOSE
Kite logo
CLIENT
Shanti Kite Products Co.
DESIGN FIRM
Sackett Design Associates
ALL DESIGN
Mark Sackett, Wayne Sakamoto

Logo was created by scanning a hand-drawn illustration into Adobe Photoshop and combining it with Adobe Illustrator and QuarkXPress files. Actual fabric was laid on the scanner to achieve background image. Final products include advertisements, decals, and patches.

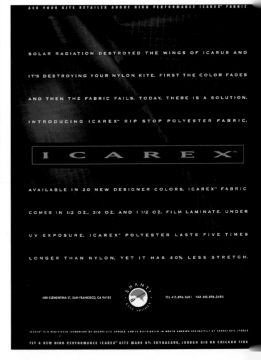

Camping, Backpacking, Hiking
PRODUCT/PURPOSE
Tents, backpacks
CLIENT
Quest
DESIGN FIRM
Sackett Design Associates
DESIGNER
Mark Sackett, Wayne Sakamoto
ILLUSTRATOR
Mark Sackett, Wayne Sakamoto

Developed in Adobe Illustrator and
QuarkXPress, this logo was used for
a 4-color process advertisements, 2-
color process woven labels, and for
multi-color applications on products
and collateral brochures.

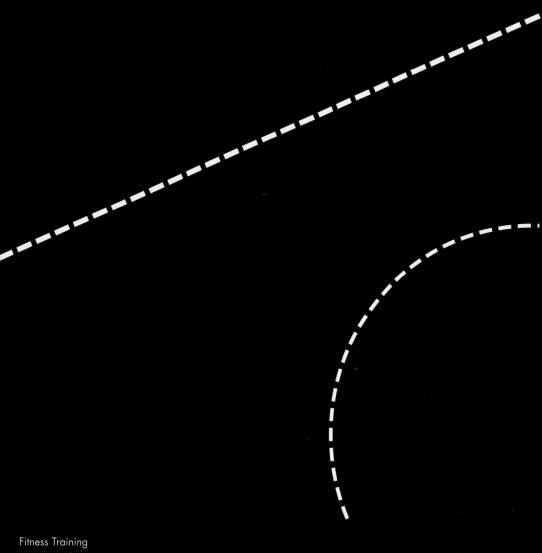

Fitness Training
PRODUCT/PURPOSE
FIT @ SUN fitness center identity
CLIENT
Sun Microsystems, Inc.
DESIGN FIRM
Earl Gee Design
ART DIRECTOR
Earl Gee
DESIGNER
Earl Gee, Fani Chung
ILLUSTRATOR
Earl Gee

The figure was drawn freehand, and the
typography was computer-generated. The
brochure design involved offset lithography,
while T-shirts and coffee mug logos were
screen-printed.

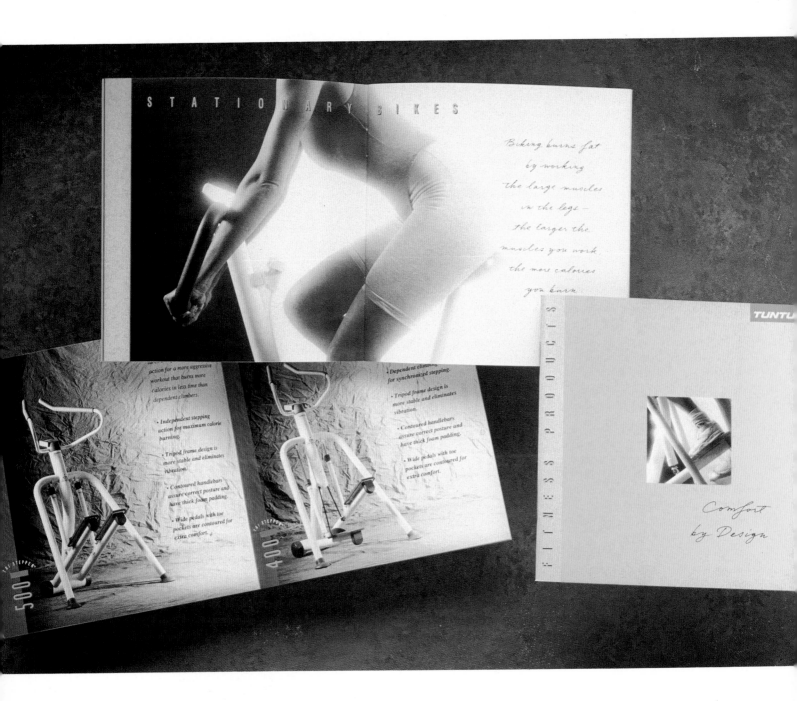

Fitness Training
PRODUCT/PURPOSE
Fitness equipment
CLIENT
Tunturi
DESIGN FIRM
Hornall Anderson Design Works
ART DIRECTOR
Jack Anderson
DESIGNER
Jack Anderson, David Bates, Paula Cox,
Mary Chin Hutchinson

Packaging created in Aldus FreeHand and
Adobe Photoshop. The equipment catalog
was developed with Aldus FreeHand and
QuarkXPress.

Fitness Training
PRODUCT/PURPOSE
Rancho Verde Lodge
CLIENT
Rancho Verde Athletic Club
DESIGN FIRM
Swieter Design
ART DIRECTOR
John Swieter
DESIGNER
John Swieter, Jim Vogel

Logo created in Adobe Illustrator.

Sports Therapy
PRODUCT/PURPOSE
West Sound Sports Therapy logo
CLIENT
West Sound Sports Therapy
DESIGN FIRM
Swieter Design
ART DIRECTOR
John Swieter
DESIGNER
John Swieter, Jim Vogel

Created in Adobe Illustrator, the identity
of the hurdler symbolizes both sports
and rehabilitation.

Fitness Training
PRODUCT/PURPOSE
Workout clothing logo
CLIENT
Workout Express
DESIGN FIRM
Hornall Anderson Design Works
ART DIRECTOR
Jack Anderson
DESIGNER
Jack Anderson, Brian O'Neill

Design created with hand-drawn
illustration and traditional typeset.

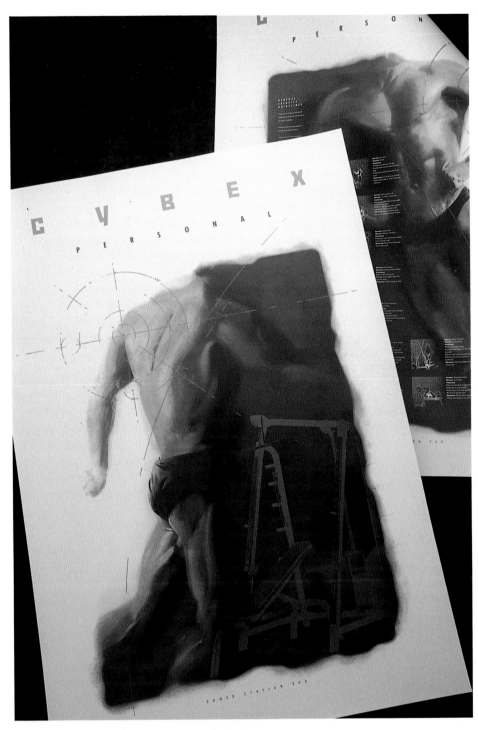

ness Training
ODUCT/PURPOSE
ength testing/rehabilitation equipment
alog
ENT
bex
SIGN FIRM
rnall Anderson Design Works
T DIRECTOR
k Anderson
SIGNER
k Anderson, David Bates,
f McClard, Julie Keenan
OTOGRAPHER
rrell Peterson

sign was created in Aldus FreeHand.

Body Building
PRODUCT/PURPOSE
Corporate logo
CLIENT
Fitness Concepts
DESIGN FIRM
Warren Group
ART DIRECTOR
Linda Warren
DESIGNER
Laura Mische

Design drawn in Adobe Illustrator.
Logo was printed by lithography.

PERFORMANCE
FITNESS CONCEPTS

Fitness Training
PRODUCT/PURPOSE
Shipboard fitness club identity
CLIENT
Holland America Line Westours, Inc.
DESIGN FIRM
Hornall Anderson Design Works
ART DIRECTOR
Juliet Shen
DESIGNER
Juliet Shen, Heidi Favour
ILLUSTRATOR
John Fretz

Design was created by hand with
traditional illustration and typeset.

Fitness Training
PRODUCT/PURPOSE
Cross training shoe, shoe box
CLIENT
FILA Footwear USA, Inc.
DESIGN FIRM
Kornick Lindsay
ART DIRECTOR
Sandy Krasovec

The character was drawn freehand,
and the logotype was screen-printed
on the boxes.

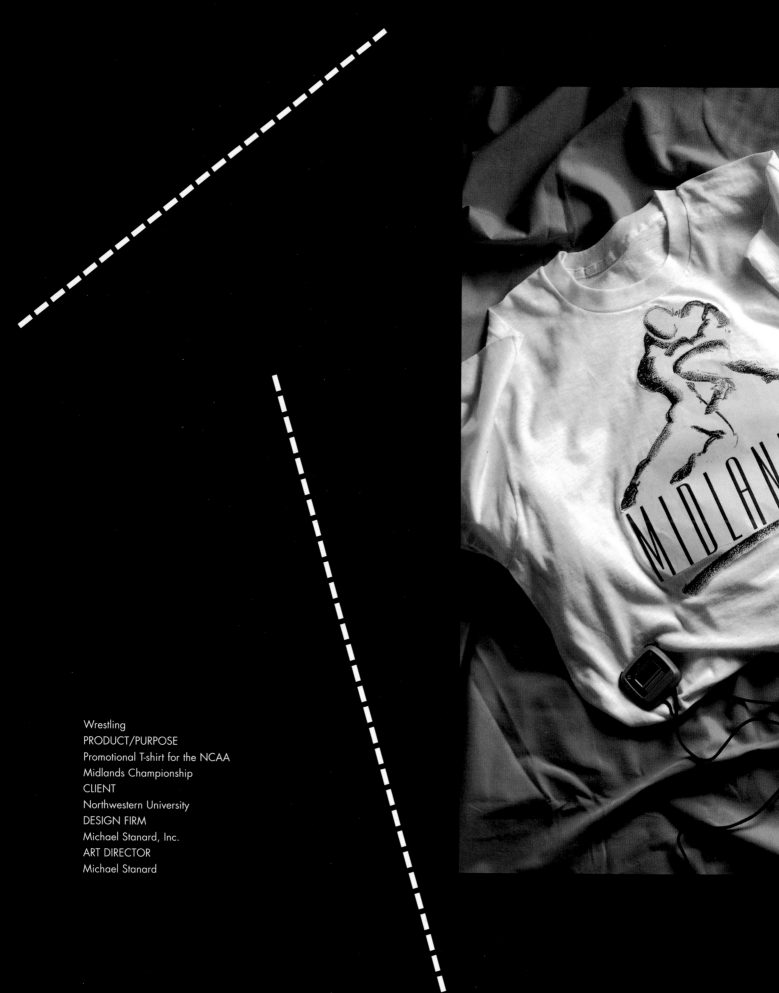

Wrestling
PRODUCT/PURPOSE
Promotional T-shirt for the NCAA
Midlands Championship
CLIENT
Northwestern University
DESIGN FIRM
Michael Stanard, Inc.
ART DIRECTOR
Michael Stanard

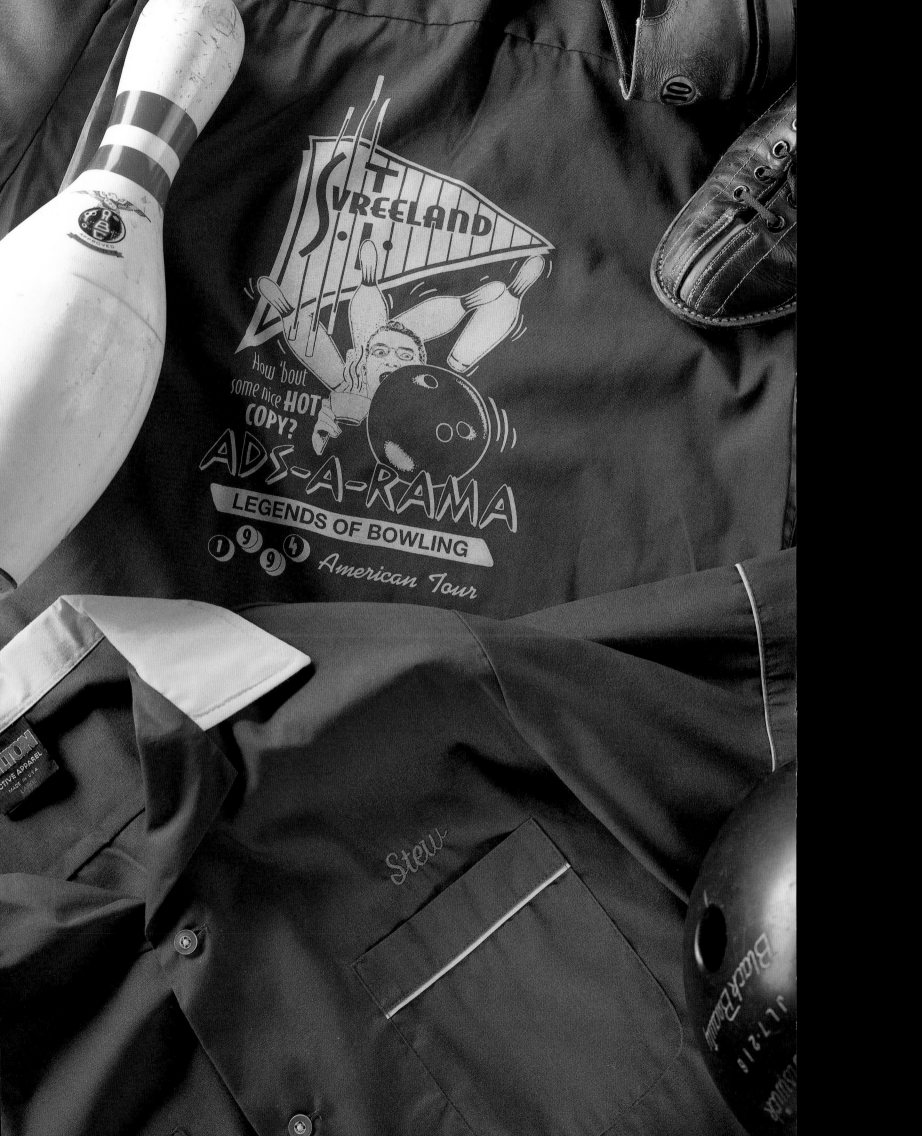

vling
ODUCT/PURPOSE
vling team uniforms
ENT
Vreeland
SIGN FIRM
Vreeland
DIRECTOR
wart Vreeland
SIGNER
wart Vreeland, Tom Hubbard
USTRATOR
wart Vreeland, Tom Hubbard

work created with ink Xerox
computer laser prints,
screening, and embroidery.

Running
PRODUCT/PURPOSE
Raise the Roof Fun Run logo
CLIENT
Arlington Museum of Art
DESIGN FIRM
Swieter Design
ART DIRECTOR
John Swieter
DESIGNER
Jenice Heo

Logo created in Adobe Illustrator.

Baseball
PRODUCT/PURPOSE
Diamonds Are Forever Invitation fund-
raising event invitation
CLIENT
Arlington Museum of Art
DESIGN FIRM
Swieter Design
ART DIRECTOR
John Swieter
DESIGNER
John Swieter, Mark Ford, Jenice Heo

These invitations, encouraging artists to
donate renderings related to baseball,
were created in Adobe Illustrator and
Adobe Photoshop.

Football
PRODUCT/PURPOSE
World Cup USA 1994 identity
CLIENT
World Cup 1994 Organizing Committee
DESIGN FIRM
Pentagram Design
ART DIRECTOR
Michael Gericke, Woody Pirtle
DESIGNER
Michael Gericke, James Anderson

Created by hand with a multitude of sketches, then refined and executed in Adobe Illustrator on a Macintosh computer.

American Football
PRODUCT/PURPOSE
25th Anniversary Commemorative logo,
celebrating OSU's football championship
CLIENT
Ohio State University
DESIGN FIRM
Rickabaugh Graphics
ALL DESIGN
Eric Rickabaugh

The logo was created in Aldus FreeHand and
has been applied to posters, T-shirts, hats, and
sweat shirts, using embroidery and offset and
screen-printing.

American Football
PRODUCT/PURPOSE
OSU autographed football
CLIENT
Ohio State University
DESIGN FIRM
Rickabaugh Graphics
ART DIRECTOR
Eric Rickabaugh, Mark Krumel
DESIGNER
Michael Smith

The logo was created using cut Rubylith film and the football was screen-printed with a 3-color method.

Sailing
PRODUCT/PURPOSE
Sailboat race merchandising items
CLIENT
Texaco Do Brazil S/A
DESIGN FIRM
Animus Comunicação
ART DIRECTOR
Rique Nitzsche

DESIGNER
Felício Torres
ILLUSTRATOR
Felício Torres

CorelDraw 4.0 software was used to create the design, which was then silk-screened. The material was created for a 24-hour sailboat race on Lagoa Rodrigo de Freitas in Rio De Janiero, sponsored by Texaco Do Brazil S/A.

Running Marathon
PRODUCT/PURPOSE
Promotional T-shirt
CLIENT
Clairol
DESIGN FIRM
Mike Quon Design Office
ART DIRECTOR
Mike Quon, Scott Fishoff
ALL DESIGN
Mike Quon

Illustration done by hand, scanned into the computer, and colored in Adobe Illustrator 5.5. Design was printed on products with a silk-screen process.

Winter Olympics
PRODUCT/PURPOSE
1992, 1994 Winter Olympics identity
for CBS network coverage
CLIENT
CBS Sports
DESIGN FIRM
Pentagram Design
ART DIRECTOR
Michael Gericke
DESIGNER
Michael Gericke, Nic Stuckey

Sketched by hand, then refined and
executed in Adobe Illustrator on a
Macintosh computer.

Tennis
PRODUCT/PURPOSE
Mental Health Association Shoot
Out 1994 promotional poster
CLIENT
Mental Health Association of
Greater Dallas
DESIGN FIRM
SullivanPerkins
ART DIRECTOR
Art Garcia
DESIGNER
Art Garcia, Melissa Witt
PHOTOGRAPHER
Russ Adams

Offset printing was used in the
design process.

Tennis
PRODUCT/PURPOSE
U.S. Tennis Association
Tournament promotional items
CLIENT
Cellular One
DESIGN FIRM
Hornall Anderson Design Works
ART DIRECTOR
Jack Anderson
DESIGNER
Jack Anderson, David Bates
ILLUSTRATOR, POSTER
John Fortune, Scott McDougall
ILLUSTRATOR, T-SHIRT
Julie LaPine, Brian O'Neill

Design created with a hand-
drawn illustration and a
calligraphic brushstroke.

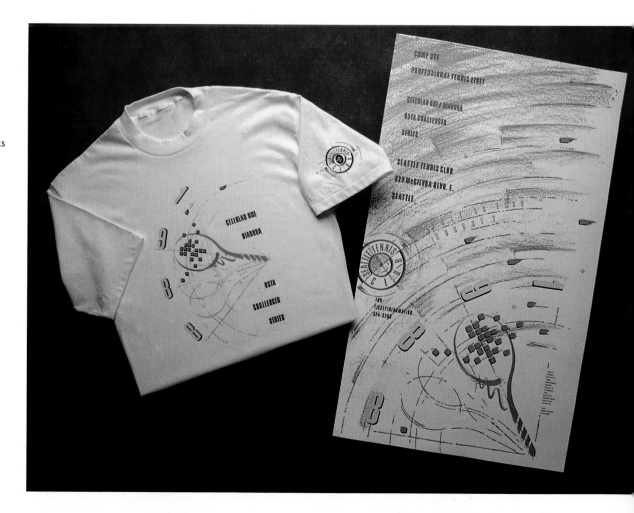

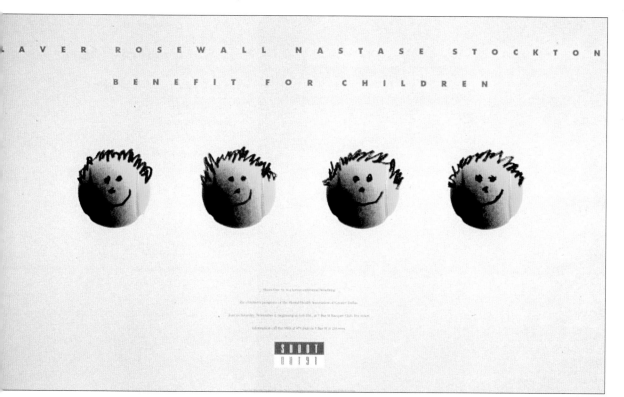

Tennis
PRODUCT/PURPOSE
Mental Health Association Shoot
Out 1994 promotional poster
CLIENT
Mental Health Association of
Greater Dallas
DESIGN FIRM
SullivanPerkins
ART DIRECTOR
Art Garcia
DESIGNER
Art Garcia, Melissa Witt
PHOTOGRAPHER
Russ Adams

Photography and offset printing
were integral to the logo design.

Tennis
PRODUCT/PURPOSE
Mental Health Association Shoot
Out 1994 promotional poster
CLIENT
Mental Health Association of
Greater Dallas
DESIGN FIRM
SullivanPerkins
ART DIRECTOR
Art Garcia
DESIGNER
Art Garcia, Melissa Witt
PHOTOGRAPHER
Russ Adams

Image was created with desktop
software and offset printing.

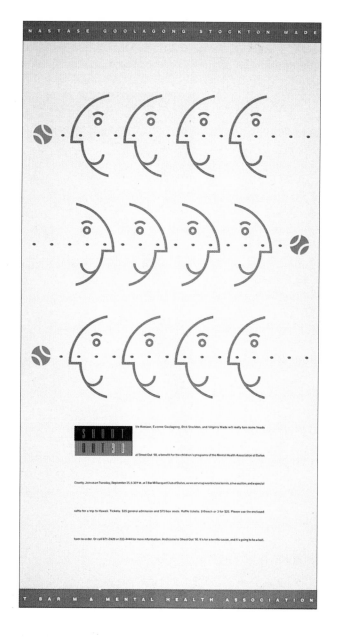

Hockey
PRODUCT/PURPOSE
NHL event program cover
CLIENT
Quality Color Press/Edmonton Oilers
DESIGN FIRM
Gerard Graphics
ALL DESIGN
Gerard Blommaent

Logo was created with airbrushing techniques, Dr. Ph. Martin dyes, pencil and ink, and gauche.

Aerobics
PRODUCT/PURPOSE
Fund-raising items for
Sick Kids Hospital, Toronto
CLIENT
Toronto Sick Kids Hospital
DESIGN FIRM
The Riordon Design Group Inc.
ALL DESIGN
Dan Wheaton

This was part of a group of products designed for a telethon to raise money for the hospital. Original design was created on scratchboard, then scanned in Adobe Illustrator, altered in Adobe Photoshop, and colored with different schemes for different items.

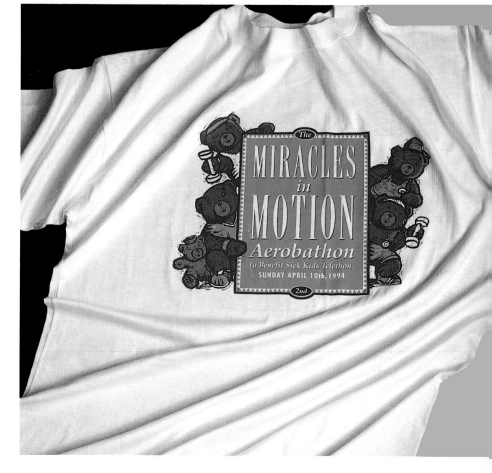

Baseball
PRODUCT/PURPOSE
Sales performance award
CLIENT
ServiceMaster of Canada
DESIGN FIRM
The Riordon Design Group Inc.
ART DIRECTOR
Ric Riordon

DESIGNER
Dan Wheaton, Ric Riordon
ILLUSTRATOR
Dan Wheaton

These baseball shirts, based on the Spring
Break campaign, were presented for top
sales achievements for the spring quarter.
Pizza boxes were used as economical
packaging.

Cricket
PRODUCT/PURPOSE
The Ashes celebration invitations,
menus, mementos
CLIENT
The Australian Cricket Board
DESIGN FIRM
Cato Design Inc
ALL DESIGN
Ken Cato

To achieve the effect of burnt edges,
the invitations and menus were individ-
ually crafted using a blow torch.

Olympic Games
PRODUCT/PURPOSE
1996 Melbourne Olympics identity candidature
CLIENT
Melbourne Olympic Committee
DESIGN FIRM
Cato Design Inc
ALL DESIGN
Ken Cato

The Olympic flame was the main inspiration for this logo. The design was featured on T-shirts, banners, and flags.

Olympic Games
PRODUCT/PURPOSE
1996 Melbourne Olympics identity candidature
CLIENT
Melbourne Olympic Committee
DESIGN FIRM
Cato Design Inc
ALL DESIGN
Ken Cato

These city decorations include a series of large,
free-standing metal sculptures painted in primary
Olympic colors. The graphics appeared on banners and flags as well.

Football
PRODUCT/PURPOSE
World Cup merchandising
CLIENT
Produtos Alimenticios Fleischmann
e Royal Ltda.
DESIGN FIRM
Animus Comunicação
ART DIRECTOR
Rique Nitzsche
DESIGNER
Felício Torres

ILLUSTRATOR
Felício Torres

The design was drawn using
CorelDraw 4.0 software and was then
silk-screened. The creation employed
the colors of the Brazilian flag (yellow,
green, blue) and was oriented to a
cheering group of young people. This
image was used on merchandising
material for winners of a Brazilian
promotion to see the final game of
world football championship.

Football
PRODUCT/PURPOSE
World Cup 1994 ball logo
CLIENT
Adidas
DESIGN FIRM
Design Bridge Limited
ART DIRECTOR
Rod Petrie
DESIGNER
Dave Annetts

Created with desktop software on
an Apple Macintosh computer.

Football
PRODUCT/PURPOSE
World Cup Frito Lay logo
CLIENT
Frito Lay
DESIGN FIRM
Swieter Design
ART DIRECTOR
John Swieter
DESIGNER
John Swieter, Jim Vogel

Image designed in Adobe Illustrator.

SPECIAL EVENTS

135

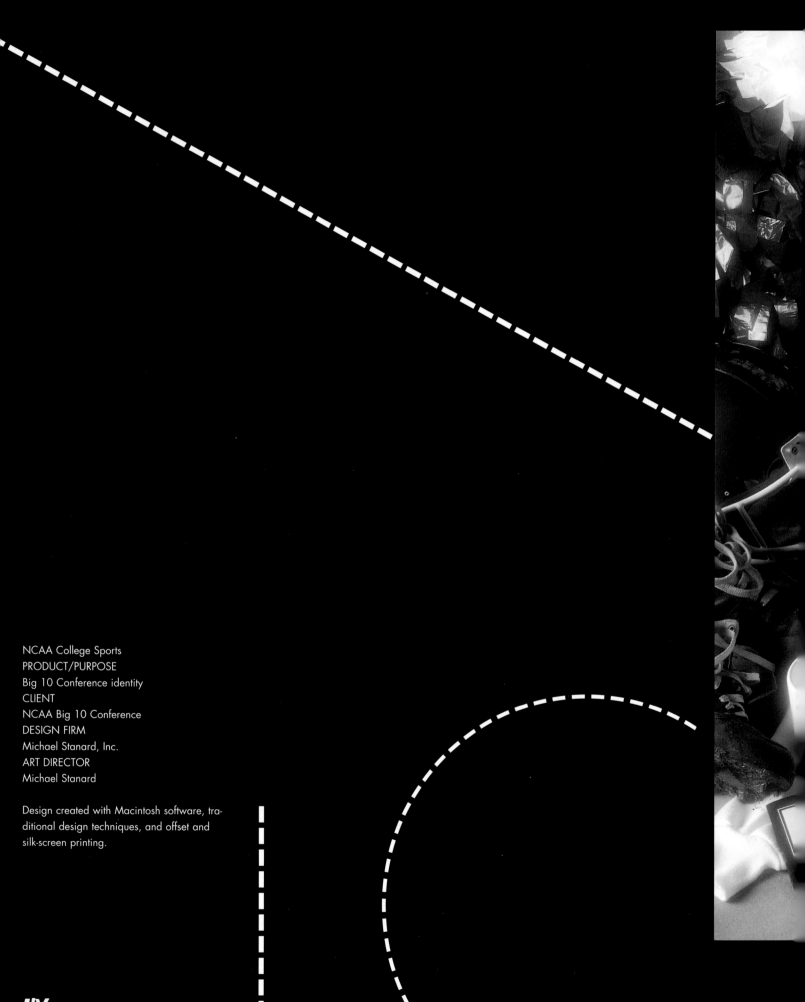

NCAA College Sports
PRODUCT/PURPOSE
Big 10 Conference identity
CLIENT
NCAA Big 10 Conference
DESIGN FIRM
Michael Stanard, Inc.
ART DIRECTOR
Michael Stanard

Design created with Macintosh software, traditional design techniques, and offset and
silk-screen printing.

PRODUCT/PURPOSE
Retail items
CLIENT
LA Gear
DESIGN FIRM
Mires Design, Inc.
ART DIRECTOR
Scott Mires
DESIGNER
Scott Mires
PRODUCTION
Miguel Perez
ILLUSTRATOR
Tracy Sabin

Logo created in Adobe
Illustrator 3.2.

PRODUCT/PURPOSE
Promotional T-shirt for
cross training athletic shoes
CLIENT
LA Gear
DESIGN FIRM
Mires Design, Inc.
ART DIRECTOR
Scott Mires
DESIGNER
Scott Mires
ILLUSTRATOR
Tracy Sabin

Design refined the "Light Gear
Man" logo and incorporated it with
type in Adobe Illustrator 3.2. Final
logo was silk-screened onto T-shirts
using a 3-color method.

PRODUCT/PURPOSE
Sporting apparel
CLIENT
JanSport
DESIGN FIRM
Hornall Anderson Design Works
ART DIRECTOR
Jack Anderson
DESIGNER
Jack Anderson, Cliff Chung, Jani
Drewfs

Design was created with conventional hand-drawn images and
traditional typeset.

PRODUCT/PURPOSE
Color logo
CLIENT
DFS Group
DESIGN FIRM
Sackett Design Associates
DESIGNER
Mark Sackett, Wayne Sakamoto
ILLUSTRATOR
Mark Sackett, Wayne Sakamoto

Logo was created in Adobe
Illustrator and QuarkXPress and
was used for a sports watch specialty store. The logo was applied
to signage and to the product.

PRODUCT/PURPOSE
Athletic clothing brochure
CLIENT
Champion, Spring City Sporting
DESIGN FIRM
Integrate, Inc.
ALL DESIGN
Darryl Levering

Photograph was scanned into
a Macintosh computer and
manipulated.

Horseshoe
PRODUCT/PURPOSE
Logo for a horseshoe tournament
CLIENT
Bucks Bar & Grill

Golf
PRODUCT/PURPOSE
Logo for golf-athon
CLIENT
Seattle ADA

Basketball
PRODUCT/PURPOSE
Three on three basketball tournament logo
CLIENT
Seattle ADA

Lacrosse
PRODUCT/PURPOSE
Team logo
CLIENT
Minneapolis Lacrosse Club

Basketball
PRODUCT/PURPOSE
Team logo for playground basketball
CLIENT
Palace Recreation Center

Hockey
PRODUCT/PURPOSE
Hockey league logo
CLIENT
West Side West End Hockey Association

DESIGN FIRM
Way Cool Creative
ALL DESIGN
Peter Winecke

Design was created with pen and
ink, using circle templates and
french curves, and then screen-
printed on T-shirts and posters.

PRODUCT/PURPOSE
Proformance letterhead
CLIENT
Proformance
DESIGN FIRM
Swieter Design
ART DIRECTOR
John Swieter
DESIGNER
John Swieter, Tim Nolly Robins
ILLUSTRATOR
Jim Vogel

The sports imagery, bold color scheme, and duotones of this letterhead were designed in Adobe Illustrator and Adobe Photoshop.

PRODUCT/PURPOSE
Dockers sweatshirt
CLIENT
Levi's Dockers
DESIGN FIRM
Sackett Design Associates
ALL DESIGN
Mark Sackett, Wayne
Sakamoto

This sports-themed line of
sweatshirts for Levi's Dockers
was created in Adobe
Illustrator and QuarkXPress.
Products were silk-screened
and puff ink printed using six
colors.

PRODUCT/PURPOSE
Label, hangtag, patch, sweatshirt
CLIENT
Levi's Dockers
DESIGN FIRM
Sackett Design Associates
ALL DESIGN
Mark Sackett, Wayne Sakamoto

All type was created using photo
typesetting and traditional paste-
up. No computers were used. All
the graphics for these Levi's
Dockers jackets, from hangtag and
label to patches, were designed
around a central sporting theme.

PRODUCT/PURPOSE
Athletic underwear packaging
CLIENT
Jockey International, Inc.
DESIGN FIRM
Lipson-Alport-Glass & Associates
ART DIRECTOR
Sam J. Ciulla
DESIGNER
Tracy Bacilek

Design created using Adobe
Illustrator. The package structure
was printed using offset
lithography printing.

PRODUCT/PURPOSE
Athletic underwear packaging
CLIENT
Jockey International, Inc.
DESIGN FIRM
Lipson-Alport-Glass & Associates
ART DIRECTOR
Sam J. Ciulla, Tracy Bacilek
DESIGNER
Amy Russell

PRODUCT/PURPOSE
Athletic underwear packaging
CLIENT
Jockey International, Inc.
DESIGN FIRM
Lipson-Alport-Glass & Associates
ART DIRECTOR
Sam J. Ciulla
DESIGNER
Carol Davis

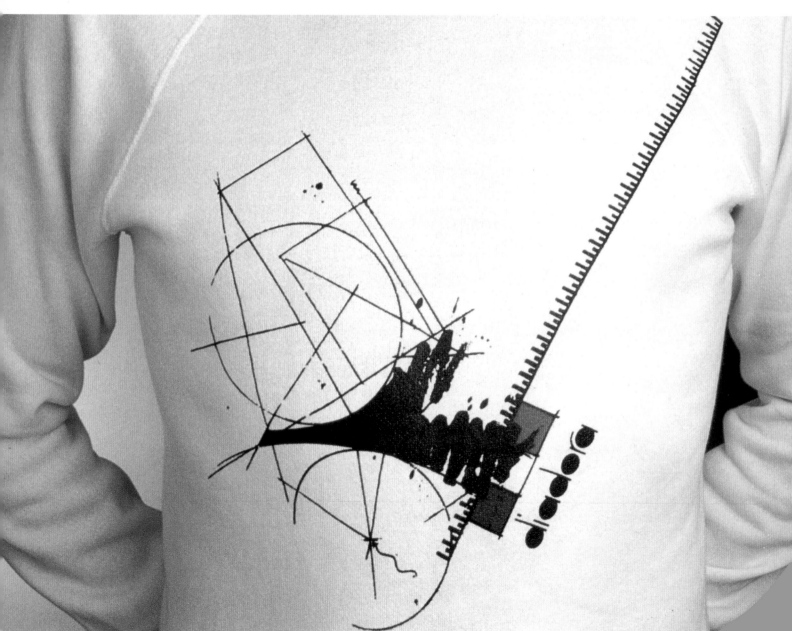

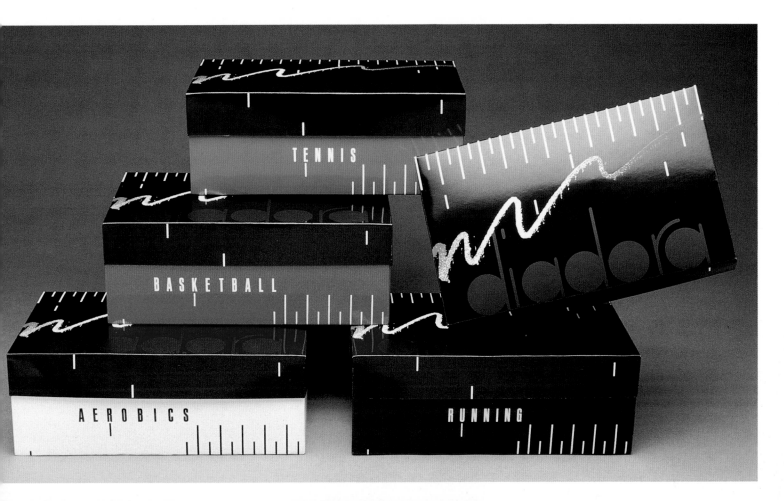

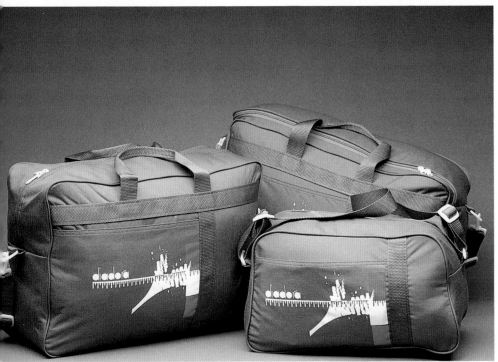

PRODUCT/PURPOSE
Athletic shoes, shoebox, clothing
CLIENT
Diadora USA
DESIGN FIRM
Hornall Anderson Design Works
ART DIRECTOR
Jack Anderson
DESIGNER
Jack Anderson, David Bates, Juliet Shen,
Cheri Huber, Mary Hermes

Design was drawn completely by hand as
a pencil sketch design.

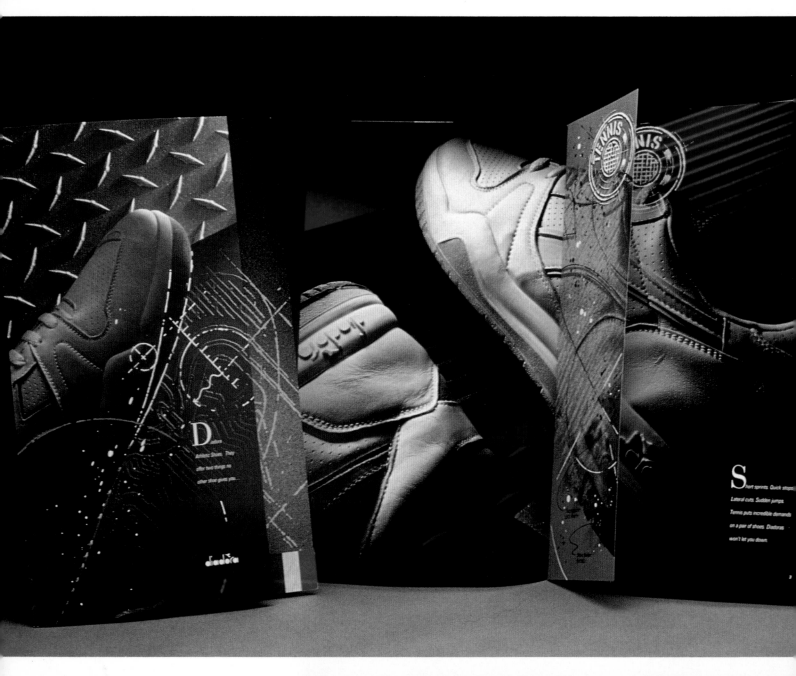

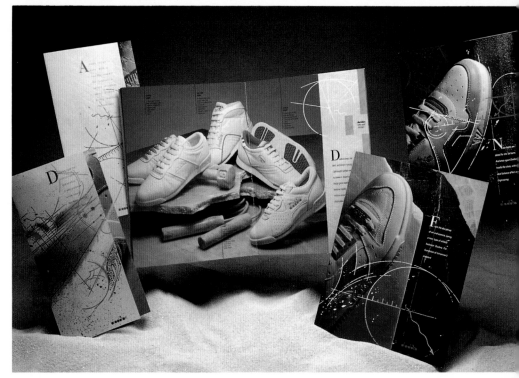

PRODUCT/PURPOSE
Athletic Shoes, shoebox
CLIENT
Diadora
DESIGN FIRM
Hornall Anderson Design Works
ART DIRECTOR
Jack Anderson
DESIGNER
Jack Anderson, David Bates, Juliet Shen

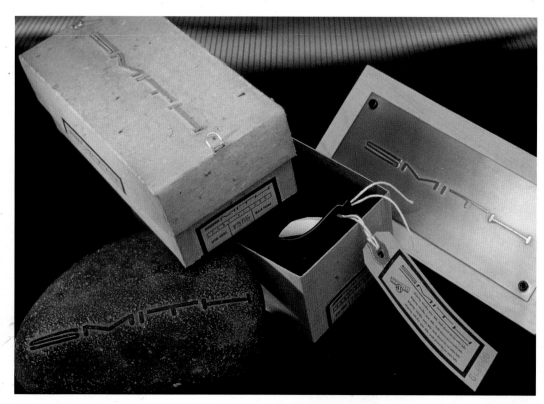

PRODUCT/PURPOSE
Sunglasses
CLIENT
Smith Sport Optics
DESIGN FIRM
Hornall Anderson Design Works
ART DIRECTOR
Jack Anderson
DESIGNER
David Bates

PRODUCT/PURPOSE
Point of purchase poster
CLIENT
Vans Shoes, Inc.
DESIGN FIRM
dGWB Advertising
ART DIRECTOR
Wade Koniakowsky
DESIGNER
Jeff Labbé
ILLUSTRATOR
Janice Lowry

Adobe Photoshop 3.0 was used
to develop this design.

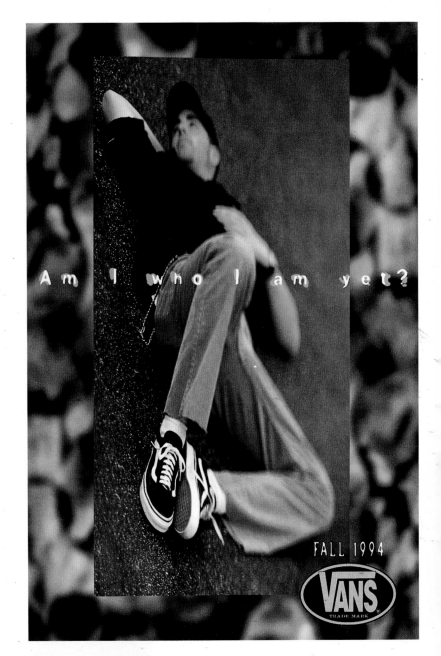

Shoes
PRODUCT/PURPOSE
Brochure
CLIENT
Vans Shoes, Inc.
DESIGN FIRM
dGWB Advertising
ALL DESIGN
Al Christensen

Brochure created with QuarkXPress 3.3
and Adobe Photoshop 2.5.

PRODUCT/PURPOSE
Sunglasses
CLIENT
Smith Sport Optics
DESIGN FIRM
Hornall Anderson Design Works
ART DIRECTOR
Jack Anderson
DESIGNER
David Bates, Cliff Chung

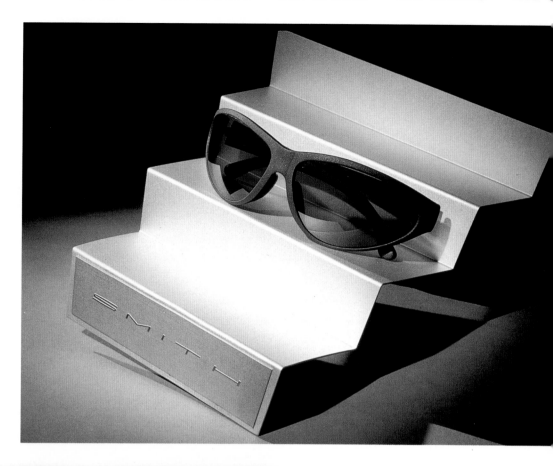

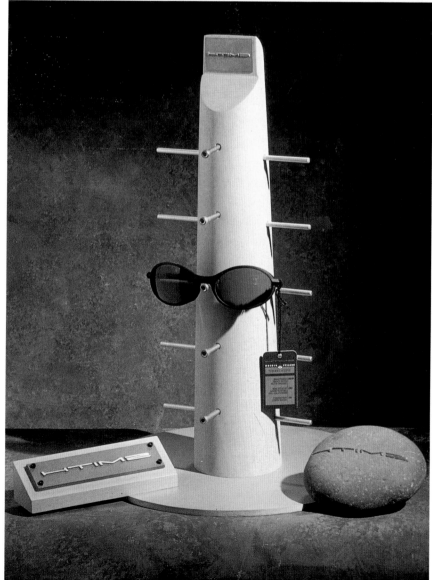

PRODUCT/PURPOSE
Sunglasses
CLIENT
Smith Sport Optics
DESIGN FIRM
Hornall Anderson Design Works
ART DIRECTOR
Jack Anderson
DESIGNER
David Bates, Cliff Chung

INDEX OF DESIGN FIRMS

IRECTORY OF DESIGN FIRMS

13th Floor
3309 Pine Avenue
Manhattan Beach, CA 90266

Alfred Design
1020 Bellevue Avenue
Wilmington, DE 19809

Animus Comunicação
Ladeira Do Ascurra
115-A/Cosme Velho
Rio De Janeiro - CEP: 22241-320
Brazil

Anspach Grossman Portugal Inc.
711 Third Avenue
New York, NY 10017

Mário Aurélio & Associados
Rua Cidade Do Reliff 232
30E 4200 Porto
Portugal

Cato Design Inc
254 Swan Street
Richmond, Victoria 3121
Australia

dGWB Advertising
20 Executive Park #200
Irvine, CA 92714

Design Bridge Limited
18 Clerkenwell Close
London EC1R 0AA
England

Design Center
School of the Arts
325 North Harrison Street
Richmond, VA 23284

Erin Edwards Advertising
42 Silvermine Road
Seymoor, CT 06483

Elton Ward Design
P.O. Box 802
Parramatta NSW 2124
Australia

Antero Ferreira Design
Rua De Roriz 203
P-Y100   Portugal

Earl Gee Design
38 Bryant Street, Suite 100
San Francisco, CA 94105

Gerard Graphics
8765 51st Avenue
2nd Floor
Edmonton AB-TGE-5H1
Canada

Hanson Associates, Inc.
133 Grape Street
Philadelphia, PA 19127

Hornall Anderson Design Works
1008 Western Avenue, Suite 500
Seattle, WA 98104

Integrate, Inc.
32 Warren Street
Columbus, OH 43215

Byron Jacobs Design
D-3, 11 MacDonnell Road
Hong Kong

Dean Johnson Design
604 Fort Wayne Avenue
Indianapolis, IN 46204

Kornick Lindsay
1 Union Square West #701
New York, NY 10003

Russell Leong Design
847 Emerson Street
Palo Alto, CA 94301

Lipson-Alport-Glass & Associates
666 Dundee Road
Suite 103
Northbrook, IL 60062

Mires Design, Inc.
2345 Kettner Boulevard
San Diego, CA 92101

NBA Properties, Inc./
Creative Services
450 Harmon Meadow Boulevard
Secaucus, NJ 07094

PPA Design Limited
D-3, 11 MacDonnell Road
Hong Kong

PandaMonium Designs
14 Mt. Hood Road,
Suite 3
Boston, MA 02135

Pentagram Design
212 Fifth Avenue
New York, NY 10010

Qually + Co. Inc.
2238 Central Street
Evanston, IL 60201

Mike Quon Design Office
568 Broadway #703
New York, NY 10012

Rickabaugh Graphics
384 W. Johnstown Road
Gahanna, OH 43230

The Riordon Design Group Inc.
1001 Queen Street West
Mississauga, Ontario L5H 4E1
Canada

Rocket Advertising Design
139B Cottonwood Avenue
Hartland, WI 53029

Sackett Design Associates
2103 Scott Street
San Francisco, CA 94115

Mike Salisbury Communications Inc.
2200 Amapola Court
Torrance, CA 90501

Clifford Selbert Design
Collaborative
2067 Massachusetts Avenue
Cambridge, MA 02140

Michael Stanard, Inc.
1000 Main Street
Evanston, IL 60202

Studio M D
1512 Alaskan Way
Seattle, WA 98101

SullivanPerkins
2811 McKinney Avenue
Suite 320, LB111
Dallas, TX 75204

Swieter Design
3227 McKinney, Suite 201
Dallas, TX 75204

Julia Tam Design
2216 Via La Brea
Palos Verdes, CA 90274

THARP DID IT
50 University Avenue
Suite 21

Los Gatos, CA 95030
Thule
42 Silvermine Road
Seymoor, CT 06483

S.T. Vreeland
P.O. Box 938
Yarmouth, ME 04096

Warren Group
622 Hampton Drive
Venice, CA 90291

Way Cool Creative
1690 Wellesley
St. Paul, MN 55105